THE SOUTHERN W...   2

CONTENTS

© Kevin Robertson (Noodle Books) and the various contributors 2008

ISBN (10) 0-9554110-7-6   (13) 978-0-9554110-7-6

First published in 2008 by Kevin Robertson
under the **NOODLE BOOKS** imprint
PO Box 279
Corhampton
SOUTHAMPTON
SO32 3ZX
www.kevinrobertsonbooks.co.uk

Printed in England by
Ian Allan Printing Ltd
Hersham, Surrey

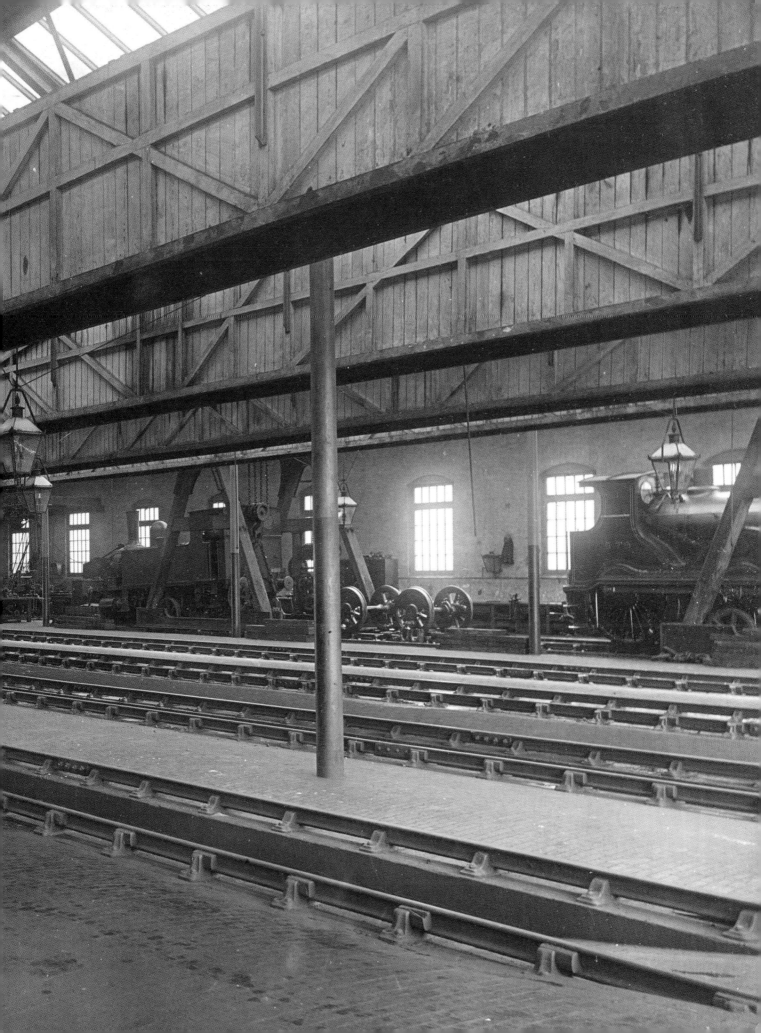

Editorial Introduction

Greetings to all and also thank you. As before I have been both humbled and amazed at the comments of so many of you following the release of Issue No 1. A number of you have also taken out subscriptions; thank you for that as well.

What has become apparent is that the Southern and indeed its constituents and successors are for the moment, at least, riding on the crest of a wave when it comes to the interest stakes.

Part of this is, of course, down to the various manufacturers, Hornby, Bachmann etc, listening to the customers and giving them exactly what they want. This, though, is bound to have a knock on effect on the kit manufacturers, but possibly a slight change of direction is required as it is unrealistic to expect the ready to run people to cater for every variation or type and consequently there may well be the opportunity for producing packs to enable variations in classes to be represented. If only someone would produce some ready to run SR 'O' gauge I would be delighted - I doubt if my wallet would be!

Returning, though, to the prototype, I am continually being asked "Where has the material for 'SW' come from?" The short answer is, certainly not all from my own collection, instead I believe it has been literally sitting on the surface waiting to be used.

Some, of course, we have purchased, other pieces we have on loan, other items we have copied or have been copied for us. Sometimes, too, things arrive unsolicited by post, I will acknowledge everything if I can, but to the person - I assume, of course, a Gentleman, who sent in a box of a dozen colour slides with just a note but no name or address and a post mark that could not be read - a special thank you.

With the amount of material we now have I can truthfully say there will be no shortage for the next few issues, likewise, of course, the Special Issue on 10201 etc., where so much arrived, I did not want it to dominate a single issue of 'SW'.

However, as before, please keep it coming. If possible I will try and give some idea when it might be used, but if more arrives on a similar subject then the result could be a re-appraisal. I regret that that is what has happened with the proposed 'SR Shipping' and 'Brighton Resignalling' articles. They will appear but bearing in mind my failure last time, all I will say is 'soon'.

Regarding history, generally, the local TV channel has recently been running a series on village life, which invariably includes items on local history. Sometimes odd snippets appear on railways and it is amazing what is still around in the way of memories as well. But these people will not be around for ever, so, if you know of someone, talk to them sooner rather than later.

For those of you also who have only joined our series at Issue No 1, you will gather that the Preview is now sold out. A reprint, though, may well be considered. If there is sufficient demand, please let me know. That way I may be able to judge when the moment is right.

Aside from the 'Special Issues' referred to, 'SW' has also spurned a potential number of other titles and I am delighted to report the schedule is for something like another eight books in 2008. Bear in mind though that in 2007 and 2006 for that matter - we did not take a holiday of any kind, so the output is dependent upon perhaps having a rest as well at some stage.

Finally, I also intend to invite guest introductions at intervals in the future. So if you would like a chance at the soapbox, let me know. Thank you again for your continued support.

Kevin Robertson

Left: - Something to get the tongues wagging! An armour plated 'Schools' recorded on 15th January 1943. The photograph (the complete of which has been reproduced) raises a number of questions. First and foremost, with the extensions the engine would certainly be prohibited from the Hastings line, whilst the obvious question is why? Discussion with others reveals a common conclusion that with the SR in closest to the enemy front line, perhaps this was an attempt to provide some protection for crews. Any other ideas would be most welcome.

John Wenyon collection

Previous page: Eastleigh running shed, with the products of Adams and Drummond visible. Although undated, the cleanliness implies the facility was relatively new and the photograph may well have been taken shortly after 1903.

Front cover: This just has to be the crew frying their breakfast - Wadebridge 1963.

Les Elsey

Rear cover: 34099 'Lynmouth' leaving Seaton Junction with the 3.10 pm to Waterloo, next stop Axminster, in March 1963.

Bruce Oliver

Memories and Recollections of the

LYMINGTON BRANCH

John Bird

"We had twenty three on the footplate for the last trip, including our two grand-daughters and the whole family! When we got to Brockenhurst, Ivan Lee said, come on Bert, we must go and have a drink! And so we ended up in the Morant Arms with a bottle of Scotch. Fortunately I had my son and daughter-in-law with me and they brought me home!"

This was how the late Bert Farley recalled his last day on the footplate, driving the last steam train from Lymington to Brockenhurst on the night of Sunday April 2nd 1967, hauled by 2-6-2T No 41312. I was privileged to interview him some twenty years later, and although he may have exaggerated the capacity of the cab of an Ivatt 2-6-2T(!), he certainly had vivid recollections of two decades operating the branch line, despite by then being just a few months away from his 84th birthday.

He probably would have been surprised to know that the line would become a home of heritage electric traction in the 21st century, another chapter in the history of an interesting, although short, branch line.

The coastal market town of Lymington,

Left: M7 Class No 30052 propels the Lymington branch train away from Brockenhurst on one of the last M7 workings, 2nd May 1964. This engine was one the final survivors of the M7 class, all of which were withdrawn by the end of same month. (Ref - PKOa-T1813)

Above: The interior of Lymington Town station shortly before steam services were ended 29th March 1967. (Ref - PSO-H7222)

N Class No 31873 shunts the daily branch freight train at Lymington Town   A Standard 2-6-0 was the more normal lunch-time visitor by 1965.   July 1965. (Ref - PT1b-C3520)

reasonably prosperous from the salt trade, had grown to a population of over four thousand by 1851 and it was just a few years later that it was linked to the national railway system. The first public passenger train from Lymington was the 7.15 am to Brockenhurst on 12th July 1858. It departed from a temporary platform a little north of the present day Lymington Town station, due to construction difficulties at the latter. At that stage, Lymington Town was to be the terminus, enabling passengers to connect with the ferry services which departed from the nearby quay to Yarmouth and later Cowes.

A railway had first been proposed in the 1840s, as a branch off Charles Castleman's Southampton and Dorchester railway. The necessary Act of Parliament was passed on 2nd July 1847, but the proposal died in the downturn following the Railway Mania. However local dignitaries under the chairmanship of brewer Alfred Mew, resurrected the scheme in 1856, and construction work began the following year.

The independent Lymington Company turned to the LSWR to operate its line, which agreed on the basis of a 50% take of the gross receipts. Thus from the start services were worked by small LSWR tank engines, such as 2-4-0T No 143 Nelson and 2-2-2T No 176 *Southampton.* Other small locos followed on until operation settled down into the hands of Beattie 2-4-0Ts in the 1880s.

By then much had changed. On 19th September 1860 the rather grand brick-built Lymington Town station was finally opened, equipped with waiting rooms, a telegraph office and bookstall. It was architecturally striking, with its patterned brickwork and round-headed windows. More importantly for passenger comfort, it featured an overall roof to protect its single platform from the coastal winds.

A small halt towards the junction with the main line was also opened at Shirley Holmes to serve local hamlets, but its existence has left few traces and it seems to have ceased to be used by the turn of the century.

The Lymington line proved quite profitable from the start and on 21st March 1879 the LSWR absorbed the independent company and set about some improvements to its infrastructure. By far the greatest of

With a Royal Blue coach service temporarily delayed by the level crossing, Ivatt Tank, Class 2MT No 41312 departs Lymington Town and passes the signal box with a two-coach train for Brockenhurst, July 1965. With goods services withdrawn and the sidings taken out of use allied to multiple unit operation not needing to turn-around, the signal box was first downgraded to a ground-frame and finally closed in 1979. (Ref - PLO-C2207)

these was the building of a new shipping pier at the end of a half-mile extension from the Town station, including a picturesque 70 yard long iron viaduct across the River Lymington. The new Pier station ended on an embankment jutting out into the river and received its first passenger train on 1st May 1884.

Thus began the clock-like regularity of the Lymington branch, little disturbed over the subsequent 120 years, apart from changes in traction. Things might have taken a very different course had the South Western and Isle of Wight Junction railway been successful in its 1901 scheme to build a line from a junction half way along the Lymington Branch to Keyhaven Marshes, and then via a 2.5 mile tunnel under the Solent, to link up with the Freshwater-Yarmouth railway on the Isle of Wight. Fortunately for the existing line, and probably the future prosperity of Lymington, the plan foundered, despite Parliamentary approval.

The main change instead was the introduction of push-pull working in 1918, initially with LSWR T1 Class 0-4-4Ts, and then ten years later handing over to the Drummond M7s. These handsome locos were the favourites of regular branch line driver Bert Farley, who worked on the line for twenty years, latterly with his regular fireman, Ray Glassey. Together they formed one of two pairs of crews that operated the line and worked alternate turns either the early shift booking on at 5am or the late shift from 1.09 pm. In the 1950s this turn was Lymington Duty No 362 and it involved a 4am start for the fireman on the early shift, and a finish towards 11pm the following week.

Apart from the branch engine and the 2-6-0 usually rostered to the daily freight, it was only on summer Saturdays that the usual routine was disturbed. In the high summer there were return workings from London Waterloo right through to Lymington Pier.
As secondary services, they were hauled in the 1950s by locos such as Class U1 2-6-0s and D15 and T9 4-4-0s. By the mid-1950s the Schools class handled most workings, later giving way to Bulleids or Standards. Large locomotives were not normally allowed down the branch, so a Q or Q1 would often take over at Brockenhurst, while the main line loco used the small turntable at Brockenhurst prior to the return working up

The view from inside Lymington MPD.
29th March 1967. (Ref - P50-H7434)

Standard Tank, Class 4MT No 80146 waits for departure at Lymington Pier station with the 1.15 pm to Brockenhurst 29th March 1967. (Ref - PB6-H7432)

Standard Tank, Class 4MT No 80134 passes Lymington Junction with the 1.15 pm Lymington Pier to Brockenhurst 21st March 1967. The signal box here had once controlled three routes, the Lymington branch, the main line, and the route through Holmsley to Ringwood. The later closed in may 1964 whilst the box was also redundant from October 1978 when the branch connection was moved to Brockenhurst. (Ref - PB6-H4329)

to London. These through working were taken over by Crompton Type 3 diesels in 1966 and even continued after electrification with multiple-unit stock for a few years.

By then, the M7s had of course fallen by the wayside, their last strongholds were the Lymington and Swanage branches and the odd journey around the 'Old Road' between Brockenhurst and Broadstone. With the closure of that route to passenger traffic on May 2nd 1964, the M7s were finally withdrawn, No 30052 being in service on the Lymington branch that day, probably for the last time. The veterans were replaced by a mixture of Ivatt 2-6-2Ts and Standard 4 2-6-4Ts and push-pull working came to an end. The footplate crews lobbied for motor fitted Ivatts to be used, but this was turned down. As Ray said, "The push and pull days were the best. When they took that away life became a real scramble, running round at each end of the journey. Those Ivatts would have been ideal for push and pull."

However whereas Ray reckoned they would have been ideal replacements for the M7s, Driver Farley did not think much of them. Even Ray had to concede

that their high bunkers were a real problem. The fireman had to do all the coaling at Lymington shed and it was a long shovel throw from the coaling stage to get the coal into their high bunkers! In fact coaling was always an issue: at lunchtime they would try to take on as much coal as possible, stacking it all over the cab, to make sure they lasted the whole day, and to cut down the work to be done at the end of the shift.

The branch engine was stabled overnight at the small single-road engine shed beside Lymington Town station. There were no other staff employed there and as Bert said, "We were our own bosses, we did as we liked, as long as the job went on alright. We used to keep the branch engine for a week at a time, then she used to go to Eastleigh for a wash-out. We did any minor jobs, burst gauge glasses, small things that needed doing, or else if she was too bad we'd have to change her over and send for another one."

The crew had to be pretty dedicated. Bert recalled a winter's morning when he had to walk from Brockenhurst to Lymington when the roads were difficult after a snow storm. It took him over two hours

Ivatt Tank, Class 2MT No 41320 at the rear of the last steam train on the Lymington branch, headed by Standard Tank, Class 4MT No 80151, the LCGB 'Hampshire Branch Lines' tour 9th April 1967. This particular tour had started from Waterloo and in addition took in a number of suburban lines in the London area as well as using examples of almost all the surviving classes of steam motive power on the Southern Region. (Ref - PLO-H9335)

and he was absolutely exhausted when he got there. But as he said, "I might as well have stayed at home, because when I got there the points were all jammed with snow so we couldn't get out of the shed anyway!"

On another occasion, Ray was very unfortunate to have an encounter with a New Forest pony as he made his way in the early morning darkness from his Southampton home by moped to raise steam at Lymington. It was a serious accident which put him in hospital for months, but did not put him off returning to the Lymington Flyer as it was affectionately known.

The railway certainly performed an important function in an essentially rural environment. School children used it in their droves to get to school in Brockenhurst, and there were also hundreds of commuters from the Isle of Wight who travelled to work on the night shift at the Wellworthy factory on the outskirts of Lymington. The factory even had its own private station, a very basic concrete structure known as Ampress Works Halt, which opened on 1st October 1958 and continued in use for over thirty years.

The signs of railway decline could not be prevented from interrupting the cosy certainties of the Lymington line however. Like many others, Lymington goods yard was closed in the summer of 1965 and this naturally led to the withdrawal of the daily freight service. This also meant no more loco coal coming in to Lymington and so the engine rosters were revised, enabling coaling to take place at Bournemouth shed each day instead. The operation of the line now became technically a Bournemouth duty, with locos being swapped each afternoon, an Ivatt replacing the Standard which had taken over in the morning.

Soon steam days on the Lymington branch were numbered. The line was to be electrified in connection with the 3rd rail being extended to Bournemouth, and so steam was scheduled to end on 2nd April 1967. As the deadline approached, the line became rather famous, with enthusiasts travelling from all over the country to travel on what became known as Britain's last steam branch line. Ron Cover, manufacturer of replacement loco number plates, made a special headboard with a red background to proclaim the fact to the whole world. However, officialdom decreed that red was unsuitable and it was removed only to reappear with a light blue background, carried for the last few days of

Preceding page: Standard Tank, Class 4MT No 80019 near Ampress Works Halt with the 10.34am Lymington Pier to Brockenhurst 26th November1966. (Ref - PB6-F9404)

Above: Standard Tank, Class 4MT No 80146 passes Lymington Town signal box with the 3.00pm from Brockenhurst, carrying the pale blue LAST STEAM BRANCH headboard 29th March 1967. (Ref - PB6-H7537)

steam services.

And so an era came to an end, on a dull wet and miserable Sunday. A posse of enthusiasts descended on the branch to smarten up No 41312 with white painted adornments on its front end, which shared the final workings with No 41320. There was also a special red headboard made by Stuart Egbeare from Portsmouth (still in existence and reunited with No 41312 for the 2007 end of SR steam celebrations on the Watercress Line) which read LAST DAY OF STEAM with the date of the opening of the line and a very well produced version of the LSWR coat of arms.

Ray Glassey recalls, "We carried duty No 404 on the last day. We had a load of fanatics, I think they had been there all night long, with their whitewash and paint. I think they had slept in the carriages."

The event was covered by Southern Television and local journalists, and Inspector Cyril Stevens was in attendance, having to turn a blind eye to the crowded footplate no doubt. Lymington was left behind to a customary explosion of detonators, but all too soon it was over.

The Ivatt was whisked off to Nine Elms for future duties on empty stock workings at Waterloo, and left Bert drowning his sorrows in whiskey and looking forward to retirement after nearly fifty years on the railways, For young Ray it was to be an uncertain future at Eastleigh, to be followed six months later by an unhappy transfer to Brighton and eventually leaving the railways for a career with Freightliners at Millbrook.

The Lymington branch however has soldiered on regardless - a short period of operation by Hampshire DEMU units followed, while the necessary works for electrification were carried out. There was even one final steam working down the line, conductor rails now in place, and with the layout simplified at Lymington Pier and Lymington Town. Thus the LCGB's Hampshire Branch Lines Rail Tour on 9th April 1967 may have been the only topped and tailed passenger train ever seen on the branch with Standard 4 tank No 80151 leading and Ivatt No 41312 at the rear.

Since 1st June 1967 operation has been by slam-door electric units, which have themselves outlived their natural lives and so become 'heritage' units. Their survival, and indeed that of the line itself is quite remarkable, given the wholesale closure of minor routes, so Brockenhurst to Lymington was not only the last steam branch, the last haven of slam door trains, but is now arguably the only true branch line to the coast still open to passengers anywhere between Walton-on-Naze and Exmouth!

The new order at Brockenhurst. Hampshire unit DEMU (Class 205) No 1126 flanked by EMU driving trailer (ex-6PAN Class No 3031) and 2HAP Class No 6102 at Brockenhurst soon after the latter took over working of the Lymington branch, 2nd June 1967. The former PAN driving trailer had been used for conductor rail clearance trails. (Ref - PD8-J7420)

All photographs by the author. © SOUTHERN-IMAGES

www.southern-images.co.uk

Southern Images PO Box 218, ALTON, Hants. GU34 9AA

John Bird is also author of

SOUTHERN STEAM SURRENDER (Kingfisher) SOUTHERN STEAM SPECIALS (Kingfisher)
and *SOUTHERN STEAM SUNSET (Runpast)*
recollecting the end of steam on the SR in the 1960s.

An article 'The Schools and the Lymington Boats' by Jeffrey Grayer
appeared in the Preview Issue of *The Southern Way*.

For the period in question this a very modern type of view and indicates well Hermann's hobby of photography. Unfortunately he left no notes with dates or details, but the location is clearly Ashford, a Maunsell 'King Arthur' seen at the head of down 'Race Special No 3', no doubt destined for Folkestone.

A PRIVILEGED PERSPECTIVE

Hermann Lound Butler, AMI Mech E, AMI Loco E, began his career with the Southern Railway in 1929 as a Pupil in the Chief Mechanical Engineers Department. His mechanical training was centred upon the Locomotive Workshops at Eastleigh, where it was then the practice for each Pupil to maintain a record of their training as they passed between the various shops and departments.

Fortunately a number of items, both relative to and contemporary with his training and career, have survived and we have been privileged to have been granted access to this material. What these records are afford a possibly unique perspective of not only the engineering training of a Pupil on the Southern Railway but later, much behind the scenes activity on the SR, as Hermann moved up the ladder and through various appointments. In the latter category are items such as an audit of stock and facilities on the Isle of Wight system circa 1940, and a few years later an equally detailed account of every incident involving two of the 'Merchant Navy' class locomotives circa 1947. Both of these will form the basis for major articles in 'Southern Way' in the future.

In the meantime we are proud to recount a record of H L Butler's locomotive riding record, covering a three month period from July to September 1932. Locomotive riding was an essential part of the training for a Pupil Apprentice at the time and, although it cannot be confirmed, it is very likely the pupil would be encouraged to 'have a go' as skills were developed and, of course, assuming crews were agreeable.

The actual record of these footplate trips as well as his formal training was contained within a small hardback booklet, the size that would easily fit into an overall pocket and was also countersigned by various foreman from time to time the consequences of loss of such a valuable item hardly bears thinking about.

Initially the entries refer to time spent in the various 'shops', which commence week ending 5th October 1929.

Shortly afterwards, from January 1930, there was day-release at university. Possibly the first time he rode on an engine was a few months later, in September 1930, although on this occasion there is no mention of which loco was involved. Six months were then spent in the Eastleigh Drawing Office, covering the period

A later view in his office at Brighton. Following completion of his apprenticeship he joined the Locomotive Testing Section in 1935, and in 1942 was loaned to the USA Transportation Corps. Further appointments followed, both in the Motive Power Department responsible for Locomotive Maintenance and then in 1948 as Technical Assistant to the Chief Officer for Locomotive Construction and Maintenance. From 1958 he was Assistant Mechanical Engineer (General) in the CME's department. He retired after many years at BRB Marylebone Road in 1972.

October 1931 to March 1932. Finally comes the time which is the subject of this commentary, which refers to being based at the nearby Eastleigh running sheds between July and September 1932.

Despite the completeness of the record, written also in a neat and legible hand, questions are raised which are now impossible to answer. Was he attached to the same crew for much of the time, or was the instruction simply to ride with as many sets of men as possible so as to witness different handling techniques? Who also set the schedules and routes? (It is interesting to note the first day was in the local yards, no doubt 'finding his feet' on the actual footplate.)

Fortunately, too, aside from training for a career on the railway, he was also keen to photograph the scene. In consequence we are privileged to see a number of wonderful views, some possibly taken at the time of the actual footplate trips.

At the time the notes were recorded it could hardly have been imagined there would ever have been an interest in them decades later, no doubt it was for this very reason that so many similar records were discarded. Nowadays of course we know differently.

I am indebted to Howard and Linda Butler for their kindness and trust and also much welcome hospitality.

Date	Engine No	Train	Time on
Monday July 11th	53	Carriage Shunter, Eastleigh	7.30 – 3.30 pm
Tuesday July 12th	585	Light Engine Eastleigh - Salisbury	7.30 – 4.30 pm
	466	9.42 am Salisbury – Portsmouth	
	466	2.04 pm Portsmouth – St Denys	
Wednesday July 13th	440	7.46 am Eastleigh – Bournemouth	7.00 – 1.30 pm
		(left shed 7.20)	
	586	11.37 am Bournemouth - Eastleigh	7.30 – 4.15 pm
Thursday July 14th	834	8.22 am Eastleigh - Waterloo	
	1621	12.24 pm Waterloo - Basingstoke	
	571	Basingstoke - Eastleigh	
Thursday August 4th	557	10.00 am Eastleigh - Bournemouth	8.30 – 1.30 pm
		(left shed 9.40)	
	601	11.37 am Bournemouth - Eastleigh	
Friday August 5th	836	8.22 am Eastleigh - Basingstoke	7.30 – 11.00 am
	778(?)	Basingstoke – Eastleigh	
Monday August 8th	464	1.43 pm Eastleigh - Woking	1.00 – 7.30 pm
	464	4.03 pm Woking - Waterloo	
	787	5.30 Waterloo - Winchester	
	679	Winchester - Eastleigh	
Tuesday August 9th	748	7.40 am Eastleigh - Bournemouth	7.30 – 2.30 pm
	418	Bournemouth - Weymouth	
	418	11.10 am Weymouth - Bournemouth	
	661	12.42 pm Bournemouth - Eastleigh	
Wednesday August 10th	584	10.00 am Eastleigh - Bournemouth	9.30 – 5.30 pm
		(left shed 9.40)	
	788	12.32 pm Bournemouth - Waterloo	
	478	3.30 pm Waterloo - Winchester	
Thursday August 11th	836	8.22 am Eastleigh - Waterloo	7.30 – 2.30 pm
	788	12.30 pm Waterloo – Southampton	
	708	Southampton - Eastleigh	
Friday August 12th	836	8.22 am Eastleigh - Basingstoke	7.30 – 11.30 am
	738	9.45 am Basingstoke - Southampton	

Friday August 12th - Cont.	785	10.41 am Southampton - Eastleigh	*(Record signed)*
Monday August 15th	680	1.43 pm Eastleigh - Portsmouth	1.00 – 5.00 pm
	598	3.35 pm Portsmouth - Fareham	
	342	4.17 pm Fareham - Eastleigh	
Tuesday August 16th	469	8.28 am Eastleigh - Salisbury	7.30 – 6.30 pm
	405	9.30 am Salisbury – Exeter	
	452	2.26 pm Exeter - Salisbury	
	115	5.05 pm Salisbury - Romsey	
	342	5.58 pm Romsey – Eastleigh	
Wednesday August 17th	584	10.00 Eastleigh – Bournemouth	9.30 – 3.15 pm
	783	12.32 pm Bournemouth - Waterloo	
Thursday August 18th	755	11.30 am Waterloo - Winchester	11.15 am – 6.30 pm
	?	Winchester - Eastleigh	
	412	2.42 pm Eastleigh - Southampton	
	752	3.18 pm Southampton - Bournemouth	
	587	4.25 pm Bournemouth - Eastleigh	
Friday August 19th	836	8.23 am Eastleigh – Basingstoke	7.30 – 11.30 am
	862	9.45 am Basingstoke – Southampton	

'Schools' No 900 'Eton' approaching Haslemere with a Portsmouth service sometime between March 1930 and prior to electrification of the "direct" in April 1937.

Another 'Schools', this time No 932 'Blundells' alongside what is known as Canal Walk west of Fratton and having just left Portsmouth. The headcode is for a locomotive hauled service in either direction running between Waterloo and Portsmouth via Woking and Guildford.

- all photographs are from the collection of Howard Butler

Friday August 19th - Cont.		10.41 am Southampton - Eastleigh	
Monday August 22nd	156	11.56 am Eastleigh - Winchester	
	780	Winchester - Waterloo	
	755	10.30 pm Waterloo – Eastleigh (Mail)	11.45 – 12.45 pm
Tuesday August 23rd	156	11.56 am Eastleigh - Winchester	11.45 – 9.30 pm
	786	Winchester - Waterloo	
	478	7.30 pm Waterloo - Eastleigh	*(Record signed)*
Wednesday August 24th	1615	Excursion Eastleigh - Bournemouth	11.45 – 8.30 pm
	755	6.46 pm Bournemouth - Eastleigh	
Thursday August 25th	148	11.56 am Eastleigh – Winchester	11.45 – 7.15 pm
	785	Winchester- Waterloo	
	785	4.45 pm Waterloo - Southampton	
	601	6.46 pm Southampton - Eastleigh	
Friday August 26th	834	8.23 am Eastleigh - Basingstoke	7.30 – 11.30 am
	786	9.45 am Basingstoke - Southampton	
	478	10.41 am Southampton - Eastleigh	
Monday August 29th		Leave	
Tuesday August 30th	584	9.58 am Eastleigh – Bournemouth	9.30 – 2.30 pm
	792	12.32 pm Bournemouth – Southampton	
	466	1.58 pm Southampton - Eastleigh	
Wednesday August 31st	724	8.37 am Eastleigh – Southampton	8.15 – 3.45 pm
	857	8.59 am Southampton - Waterloo	
	865	1.30 pm Waterloo - Winchester	
	465	3.13 pm Winchester - Eastleigh	
Thursday September 1st	745	7.40 am Eastleigh - Bournemouth	7.15 – 11.15 am
	788	9.50 am Bournemouth - Eastleigh	
Friday September 2nd	466	8.37 am Eastleigh - Southampton	8.40 – 2.30 pm
	786	9.54 am Southampton - Waterloo	
	787	12.30 pm Waterloo - Southampton	
	466	2.01 pm Southampton - Eastleigh	
Monday September 5th	173	2.42 pm Eastleigh - Southampton	2.30 - 1.30 am
	787	3.13 pm Southampton - Bournemouth	

Monday September 5th - Cont	776	5.09 pm Bournemouth - Waterloo	
	780	9.00 pm Waterloo – Southampton Docks	
	780	1.10 am Southampton - Eastleigh	
Tuesday September 6th	680	9.58 am Eastleigh - Bournemouth	9.30 – 2.30 pm
	302	12.42 pm Bournemouth - Eastleigh	*(Record signed)*
Wednesday September 7th	835	8.23 am Eastleigh - Winchester	8.15 – 3.45 pm
	786	8.58 am Winchester - Waterloo	
	773	1.30 pm Waterloo - Winchester	
	428	3.17 pm Winchester - Eastleigh	
Tuesday September 8th	775	10.28 am Eastleigh – Basingstoke	10.15 – 2.00 pm
	523	12.30 pm Basingstoke – Winchester	
	585	3.17 pm Winchester - Eastleigh	
Friday September 9th	835	8.23 am Eastleigh – Winchester	8.15 – 1.00 pm
	791	8.56 am Winchester - Waterloo	
	857	10.30 am Waterloo – Southampton (Bournemouth Belle)	
	637	Southampton - Eastleigh	
Monday September 12th	302	8.37 am Eastleigh – Southampton	8.30 – 3.45 pm
	151	? Southampton - Salisbury	
	473	11.28 Salisbury - Waterloo	
	837	1.30 pm Waterloo - Winchester	
	663	3.17 pm Winchester - Eastleigh	
Tuesday September 13th	739	10.28 am Eastleigh - Winchester	10.15 – 2.30 pm
	781	11.12 am Winchester - Bournemouth	
	465	12.44 pm Bournemouth - Eastleigh	
Wednesday September 14th	465	8.31 am Eastleigh – Southampton	8.30 – 3.30 pm
	780	10.33 am Southampton - Bournemouth	
	792	1.26 pm Bournemouth - Southampton	
	-	3.07 pm Southampton - Eastleigh	
Thursday September 15th	835	8.23 am Eastleigh - Winchester	8.15 – 10.15 am
	792	8.56 am Winchester - Waterloo	
	473	7.30 pm Waterloo - Eastleigh	7.15 – 4.30 pm
Friday September 16th	114	8.27 am Eastleigh - Bournemouth	8.30 – 1.30 pm
	792	11.05 am Bournemouth - Winchester	
	148	1.17 pm Winchester - Eastleigh	

862 'Lord Collingwood', at Winchester waiting to depart south. Hermann rode on this engine on August 19th 1932, whilst at the head of the 9.45 am Basingstoke - Southampton service.

As seen above, Friday 16th September was the last entry in this stage of his training. It will be noted that the runs invariably commence and terminate at Eastleigh - indeed that is where he was in lodgings. Later he would tell his family his was a not a particularly happy time at Eastleigh, although whether this was related to the works or the lodgings was not explained. Both would no doubt have been a culture shock to a 19 year old in 1929, whose life before that time had been centred upon rural Stamford in Lincolnshire.

LONGPARISH

circa 1900

Anyone who has ever attempted to search for a photograph of a particular station or locomotive will know that certain locations and machines can prove elusive. Early views of Longparish certainly fall into that criteria, as whilst there are a number of well known views of neighbouring and, to be fair, similar looking Wherwell station, Longparish has probably only ever been seen previously after the track had been singled and the up platform and canopy demolished.

The story of the short connecting route from Hurstbourne through Longparish and Wherwell to Fullerton has been adequately told in other publications and will not be repeated here, suffice to say that the station, as shown, only survived in this form from 1885 to around 1913 and as such this may be considered to be a rare view.

The scene is looking north (east) towards Hurstbourne, with seven men, two children and a dog visible. These, who can be named with certainty, are standing between the platforms and are left to right, Mr Ball, Joseph Burrows, Mr Purver, and Thomas Cook Platelayer. The identity of what are probably station staff on the platform and likewise the two children is not confirmed but see below. What is known is that, according to census records railway staff in the area in 1891 and living in property in the station yard, were George Webb Platelayer, Edward Tubb 'Ganger / Platelayer', and Henry Grace 'Ganger of Platelayers'. The Station Master at the time was either Samuel Oakford or Robert Hobbs, the former in post in 1891 and the latter having replaced him by 1901. Also by 1901 Messrs Grace and Webb were no longer resident in their previous locations and instead there is reference to William Hewitt, a Porter and William Sammules Signalman. Interestingly, in 1891 there is no reference to a signalman although a porter, William Chant was referred to but living elsewhere.

The photograph came to us from Trevor Skeates, Great-Grandson of Joseph Burrows 2nd from left. Mr Burrows had been born in Salisbury in 1854 and in 1876 married his first wife Annie (nee Lawes). Five years later he is shown on the 1881 census as living at 2 Finchs Court, Salisbury and with the occupation of bricklayer's labourer. Joseph and Annie had a daughter Emma and son Alfred. Annie died in the early part of 1882.

Joseph later married again, to Jane (nee Ferbrache) and, between 1883 and 1902, they would have eight further children. By 1891 the census of that year showed Joseph working as a Platelayer and living at Station Yard, Longparish. He was still in the same occupation in 1901 although this time the address had varied very slightly to become Station Cottages. Possibly this was exactly the same location but now referred to with a different name.

Sometime between 1901 and 1915 Joseph left the railway for good, possibly to work with Charles Skeates, an Andover builder who also ran the Andover Union Workhouse. Two of Joseph's sons died whilst serving with the armed forces, Lance-Corporal Charles Edward Burrows of the Hants Regiment was killed at the age of 29, on the 27th April 1915 at Ypres whilst Alfred Henry Augustus drowned at sea on the 22nd October 1926, in the sinking of HMS Valerian in the Bermuda hurricane, he was then aged 24. Joseph Burrows himself survived to be an octogenarian.

The staff detail for the period is most interesting and throws up two totally different possibilities. One of these is the commonly held perception that staff moved around upon promotion / transfer, although the fact that the main subject of the view, Joseph Burrows, left the railway also implies that perhaps the previously held perspective of a secure and long lasting employment with the railway was not always strictly applicable.

The view is possibly the first to show Longparish signal box and also the repeating arms of the up home signals. The original goods yard, later extended in the 1940s, was located beyond the up platform to the left hand side. Singling of the main line through the station took place from 13th July 1913.

Photograph and family notes courtesy of Trevor Skeates. With grateful thanks also to John Coles.

WOOLSTON 1889

Initially, from the time of opening in March 1866, the wayside station at Woolston on the route from St Denys to Netley, possessed just a single platform. Later in September 1889 the route was extended east from Netley through to a junction at Fareham and in consequence took on a new importance with through trains between Southampton and Portsmouth. Later still in 1901 a passing loop was added whilst the route itself was doubled in May 1910. It remains in use today, although with Woolston very much a suburb of Southampton compared with the hamlet of the 19th century.

The photograph dates from June 1889, in single track days, and is viewed looking west (up) towards Bitterne and St Denys. The check rail will also be noted on what was a tight 13 chain radius curve.

On the reverse are recorded details of the Station 'Superintendent', J T Etheringham, whose place of residence was given as 'Westbournes', Portsmouth Road, Woolston. To the extreme right, with his hand on the top spar of the barrow, is the only other member of staff who can be identified Sidney Callen, the Grandfather of Sheila Rodwell, to whom we are indebted for the loan of this photograph.

The detail under the canopy is wonderful and includes poster boards for the LSWR, Midland, and Great Northern companies, as well as advertisements for 'Summer Train Health Resorts' and 'Market Tickets'.

Of similar interest is the variety of goods visible, including what appear to be at least seven crates, of butter some of which are branded S J Wight, Wellington, Somerset.

FLASHBACK

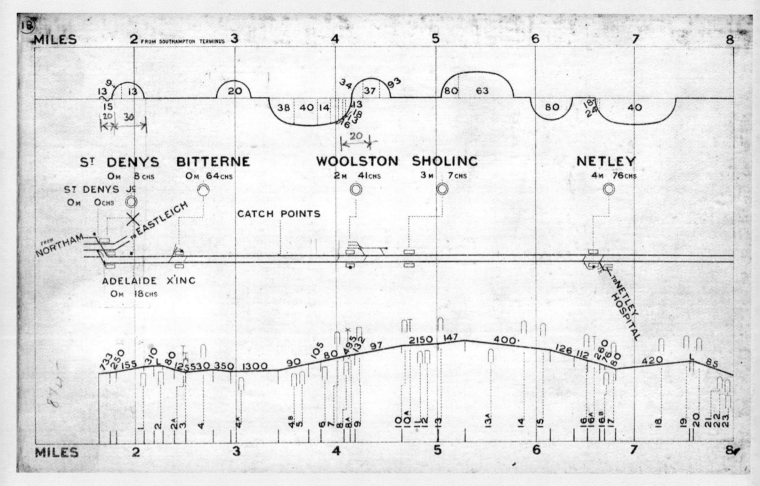

Taken from the LSWR book of system-maps, Circa 1914, the curvature of the route can be gauged. By now of course the station had reached its zenith so far as development was concerned although a siding serving a local tip was laid into the down line between Bitterne and Woolston in the 1950s.

Although seen elsewhere, the detail in the lower view, added to its relevance to the accompanying text, makes this view of the bridge just west of the station worthy of inclusion. Here was the end of what was the passing loop and bridge No 8 (over what is appropriately known as Bridge Road). This particular bridge was rebuilt in 1903/4 and with the photograph then probably dating from that time. The points to the right led to a siding, access to which is protected by the ground signal. The extreme curvature of the line can also be gauged after the end of the platform, which takes the railway around the eastern shoreline of the River Itchen.

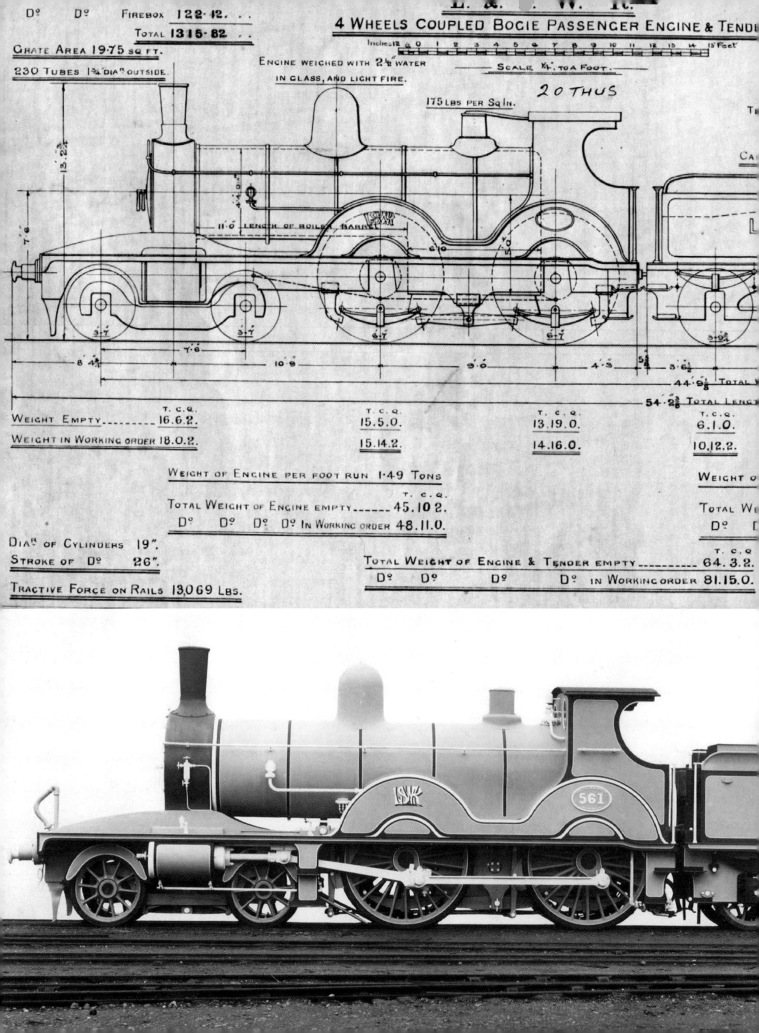

Dᵒ Dᵒ FIREBOX 122·12 · ·

TOTAL 1315·82 · ·

L. & . W. R.

4 WHEELS COUPLED BOGIE PASSENGER ENGINE & TENDER

GRATE AREA 19·75 SQ FT.

230 TUBES 1¾ DIAᵒ OUTSIDE.

ENGINE WEIGHED WITH 2½ WATER
IN GLASS, AND LIGHT FIRE.

Inches 12 9 0 1 2 3 4 5 6 7 8 9 10 11 12 13 14 15 Feet

SCALE ¼ʺ TO A FOOT.

20 THUS

175 LBS PER SQ IN.

13·2¾

7·6

11·0 LENGTH OF BOILER BARREL

6·10

3·7 3·7 6·7 6·7 3·9¼

8·4½ 7·6 10·9 9·0 4·3 5⅜ 3·6½

44·9⅝ TOTAL

54·2⅜ TOTAL LENGTH

	T. C. Q.		T. C. Q.		T. C. Q.		T. C. Q.
WEIGHT EMPTY	16.6.2.		15.5.0.		13.19.0.		6.1.0.
WEIGHT IN WORKING ORDER	18.0.2.		15.14.2.		14.16.0.		10.12.2.

WEIGHT OF ENGINE PER FOOT RUN 1·49 TONS

T. C. Q.
TOTAL WEIGHT OF ENGINE EMPTY 45.10 2.

Dᵒ Dᵒ Dᵒ Dᵒ IN WORKING ORDER 48.11.0.

WEIGHT O

TOTAL WE

Dᵒ D

DIAᵐ OF CYLINDERS 19ʺ.

STROKE OF Dᵒ 26ʺ.

T. C. Q.
TOTAL WEIGHT OF ENGINE & TENDER EMPTY 64. 3. 2.

Dᵒ Dᵒ Dᵒ Dᵒ IN WORKING ORDER 81.15.0.

TRACTIVE FORCE ON RAILS 13,069 LBS.

LSWR 561

(557-576)

EIGHED WITH TANK
FULL, NO COAL.

F TANK 3300 GALLONS.

S W R

3.9¼   3.9¼

6.6   4.9½

BUFFERS

T.C.Q.	T.C.Q.
6.13.0.	5.19.0.
10.12.2.	11.19.0.

R PER FOOT RUN 1.55 TONS.

	T.C.Q.
TENDER EMPTY	18.13.0.
² Dº IN WORKING ORDER	33.4.0.

TYPE 4-4-0.

Purely by chance...

Some months ago I had the good fortune to meet up with a gentleman in the Midlands who advised he had some material, ephemera, photographic, and hardware, which I might care to view in case any was of use in 'SW'. An appointment was duly made and hospitality greatly appreciated. (Who says railway research cannot be enjoyable as well?)

Amongst the items I was shown was a number plate from 'E561', an Adams T3 4-4-0 withdrawn back in 1930. This I duly photographed at the time with the aim of perhaps using the view to fill an otherwise empty space at the bottom of a page in a future issue. (Number-plates from this period are in themselves rare and consequently extremely valuable, and it is intentional that no clue is being given as to the owners' details.)

There matters rested, until a few months later I was fortunately successful in bidding for a quantity of LSWR material at the summer 2007 Wickham Railway Auction. Amongst the items obtained in this way were a view and likewise weight diagram of No 561. To be honest whilst the photograph may have been seen before, the diagram has not and thus the pieces fit together to complete another small piece of knowledge in the vast story of railway history.

Aside from photographs, the number-plate shown is probably the only tangible item remaining from the engine, although sister machine No 563 does survive as part of the National collection.

561's history has also been recounted by Bradley and will only be surmised here. Built at Nine Elms in February 1893, the engine was subject to minor modifications and received the plate shown complete with the 'E' prefix in October 1924. No E561 also had the melancholy distinction of being the first of the class to be withdrawn in October 1930.

Do you have a railway relic able to be photographed and the story to go with it? - pieces such as this would be very welcome.

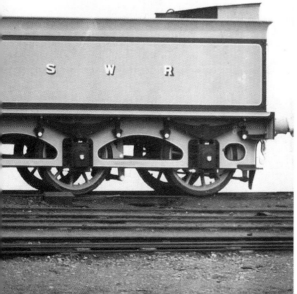

C2 No 552 - later - 2552 - on the turntable at Three Bridges, 30th April 1932. Later rebuilt and reclassified as C2X class, this engine was based at Three Bridges during Norman's time at the shed.

H C Casserley

Boat train from Newhaven to Victoria passing Three Bridges in 1949 behind 'H2' 4-4-2 'St Albans Head'.

Norman Denty collection

The Author's royalties from this article are being paid to the 'Brighton Atlantic' fund.

"THE *SWAYING* FOOTPLATE"

Part 1 of former Southern Railwayman Norman Denty's experiences in the Traffic and Locomotive departments.

In April 1940 I started work on the Southern Railway as a Messenger Boy, dressed in smart black uniform and "peaked cap". I was with the Central Dispatch Department which, because of the bombing blitz on London, had moved with its office staff to Brighton. The new home was the disused wheel shops in the locomotive works, the ground and first floors of the old shops having been hastily converted for office use. Not long after this move came Dunkirk and with it the fear of the axis armies invading the south coast of England. Accordingly the offices that had been evacuated to Brighton now returned to London Bridge Station, to a nine storey building at the end of Platforms 18-22. This had originally been the LBSCR Hotel. I, along with three other Messenger boys, who had started with me, now travelled daily from our homes in Brighton to London.

On Saturdays we worked until 12:30pm, but then, along with three other messengers who lived in London, we would go to Waterloo Station and become Porters for the afternoon. This was allowed by the management simply because we wore uniforms. In the summer of 1940, holiday makers were still going in their thousands to the resorts on the Isle of Wight, Hampshire, Dorset, Devon and Cornwall, all served by the Southern. This may seem hard to believe after the evacuation of Dunkirk, but it was nevertheless true. Probably people just wanted a break away in what they considered to be the safety of the countryside, this, of course, was before the start of the 'Battle of Britain'. Trains from those counties, carrying returning travelers, arrived continually on Saturday afternoons and we Porters would line up on the platform from end to end. We also all found jobs carrying luggage. Sometimes business was so good that we could get even more in tips by going back to the same train! Indeed we Messengers could earn the same in an afternoon as our normal weekly pay, so it was well worth the effort. (These were the good old days, when tips were not taxed.)

We were also in great demand interpreting the station announcements for passengers. I once knew a Spanish lady who had lived in England for over ten years - she could not speak a word of English but got a job as a station announcer at Waterloo!

With the dark nights of the 1940 winter, the German bombers came over London and during the midday lunch breaks the Messengers would go to the top of the offices and from there look down the River Thames to the dock areas and watch the warehouses on fire from incendiary bombs. Some warehouses would burn for weeks on end, owing to the highly flammable type of materials stored inside. Messenger work also consisted of rolling off printed notices from the 'Roneo' hand machines, which, with other letters, were sent to all stations on the Southern Railway system. Letters for the 'Foreigners' main line stations in London, the GWR, LMS and LNER, went by road transport or occasionally, if it was urgent, we would take them.

Quite often it was difficult to get to work at

Portrait of a happy man. The author alongside Schools class No 924 in 1944. The photo was taken by another Fireman, Ron Stoneman with whom Norman shared lodgings.

London Bridge, owing to the railway lines beyond Norwood having been damaged by air raids. If this was the case, once the train had reached East Croydon, it would be diverted to Victoria. From there the Messengers from Brighton would go by tube to London Bridge. One particular day, 14th December 1940, the tracks above Norwood Junction were blocked, so the trains were now routed to Victoria. We reached Balham Station but the tracks beyond this had also been bombed. Accordingly we made for the Northern line to London Bridge but that was similarly out because of enemy action. There were no buses going to the Bridge for one reason or another, so we caught one for Westminster Bridge. On arrival there we walked to the pier on the river and boarded a river bus, with a London transport conductor collecting the fares We left the water bus at Tower Pier then walked through Billingsgate fish market and on over the old London Bridge to the station, by now somewhat late for duty. Fortunately the management knew of the problems the Brighton lads had getting to work so were just pleased to see us arrive. Sadly, a large number of civilians sheltering at Balham underground station were killed that morning.

Getting home again was just as difficult. Our day normally ended at 5.00 p.m. but, if there were no trains from London Bridge, that meant using the tube for Victoria, contacting that station first by telephone to see if the trains were running. Somehow we always managed to get back to Brighton, even though it was often late at night. I shall not forget the night when our train was slowly going forward near Croydon and then stopped. The bombs were literally whistling down, the search lights flashing up into the night sky searching for the bombers and the ack-ack guns firing at them like fury. The noise was deafening as the bombs exploded - then the carriage lights went out. We four Messenger boys lay down on the floor whilst the carriage was swaying and shaking. So were we!

By the end of November we had left the offices at London Bridge and just as well, for at the end of December they were in ruins. Luckily for the staff the building was bombed at night, but all the records were destroyed. The office personnel now took up residence above Waterloo Station.

Shortly afterwards I transferred to the Traffic Department, I was still too young for acceptance by the Locomotive Department and for the moment was employed as a signal-lad at Keymer Crossing Signal Box near Burgess Hill. This was a small, though busy box with only twenty-one levers but also a set of crossing gates. The box controlled Keymer Junction, the point of divergence for the lines to Brighton and Lewes. Two signal men lived in the houses across the tracks right opposite the box, and a third occupied the former

The interior of Keymer Crossing Signal Box. The diagram shows the Brighton line running from left to right with the 'branch' to Lewes diverging.
In addition to his role of booking boy, Norman had specific, regular weekly duties:

Monday -	*Clean the signal box windows*
Tuesday -	*Shine up the handles on the signal-levers with emery cloth*
Wednesday -	*Polish brass fittings with Brasso*
Thursday -	*Scrub out the signal box and wood floor with soap and water*
Friday -	*Walk the line, trim the signal lamps and re-fill with oil*

He recounts, "Fortunately, in view of Friday's duties, there were just three semaphore signals, the up Home, outer Home and a Distant, this latter signal over a mile from the box. I would walk to these signals carrying a can of oil, wicks and a box of matches. The oil lamps burnt twenty four hours a day, and had to be refilled on a weekly basis. If I was at the top of the ladder when an express passed below, the ground would shake. This in turn would shake the post and I would hang on for dear life!"

One of Brighton's D1 tanks, 2252, still in somewhat dirty Southern livery on 1ˢᵗ March 1950, acting as Brighton station pilot. One of the staff entrances to the Works (shown in 'Southern Way No 1 p72') can be seen on the left.

Terry Cole collection

station house across the tarmac road. From Clayton Tunnel to within four miles of Haywards Heath, the trains could be followed in both directions on an illuminated panel, indicated by a white light going out when a train was between signals; when it passed them the white light came on again. The Brighton line was controlled through semi-automatic colour lights, although the line between Spadham Lane and Lewes was semaphore-controlled with conventional block working.

My role at Keymer Crossing was to book the times of the passing trains, although I was the only lad there and if I was not present the signalman did the same job himself.

On a number of occasions during my six months in the signal box I applied for a transfer to the Loco Department, as an Engine Cleaner. Eventually this request was granted, although unfortunately it was not to be near my home at Brighton. Instead I started at Three Bridges, some 22 miles away, on 19th of May 1941. Another lad from Brighton, Ray Round, started at the same shed a week after me. Later, in BR days, Ray became heavy-weight boxing champion of British Railways.

Having started officially as 'Cleaners', we did

at times indeed clean engines but within two weeks 20-ton coal wagons started to arrive in the yard. These carried emergency supplies for the shed and were off-loaded onto an area of spare ground making a large coal dump and you've guessed it - for many weeks we were the ones tasked with this backbreaking duty. There were also no washing or shower facilities at the shed - at times I began to ask myself if I should not have remained at Keymer Crossing.

Due to the general shortage of men, we cleaners also undertook other various jobs around our shifts. which included being a boiler maker's mate, whilst at other times I was the steam-raiser - or 'lighter-upper' as we called it.

More hard manual labour ensued because at that time the coaling of engines at Three Bridges was undertaken by hand. Usually this was when we were working the 2.00 pm to 10.00 pm shift and we would assist the regular coalman on occasions when the yard was particularly busy. This involved shoveling coal out of 12 ton trucks (trucks were wood built - wagons were steel) and then up into either the bunker or tender. Not surprisingly I was all-in when I arrived home. Fortunately we were compensated financially by receiving a man's pay rate for these different tasks,

The serene setting of Rowfant the first station east of Three Bridges on the line to East Grinstead. Pictured are the down side buildings and part of the platform used by services destined for East Grinstead. The siding end on the right led from the small goods yard, a continuation of which led to a nearby brick works.   *Paul Hersey collection*

thanks to the efforts of the Union. Years later, during a lightning rail strike one morning, I was in the station buffet with 'juice rail' drivers having a cup of tea, when in came an irate commuter. On seeing a driver he recognised he spouted, "Where is your train?" The driver's answer was, "Aslef-ma train in the siding". The loyalty of that particular man was very clear.

The cleaners also cleared ashes and clinker, shoveling this waste into trucks. It was while doing this task about 10.00 am each weekday that a set of Stewarts Lane men would arrive in the yard, fill up their engine at the water crane, then move on to the disposal pit to clean the fire and so on. I would then ride on the footplate to the turntable at the other side of the shed and help the fireman turn the engine this was before the days of vacuum assistance. The driver first balanced the engine on the turntable and then it was pushed around by hand. If it was a 'King Arthur' class 4-6-0 with a six wheel tender, which weighed approximately 135 tons, the balance was critical. On one occasion I remember the engine on this turn as No 795 'Sir Dinadin', in lined green paint-work and looking immaculate. However, once the engines next went into the workshops for overhaul, that was the end of them looking smart, as they were given a coat of wartime black and never looked quite the same.

July 1941 and I had my first firing turn, right out of the blue when there was the need for a special service. A horse box had arrived at Three Bridges on the back of a passenger train from Tunbridge Wells West and urgently needed to be taken to Haywards Heath cattle market. I was cleaning engines at the time and passed fireman Doug Bates was on shed duties. The running foreman told us to get No 1907, a 'U1', still in SR green, ready, which Doug and I worked for the special of just the one horse box and a brake van - indeed the engine and tender were longer than the train!

Eighteen months from the day I started as a cleaner I had what was known as the fireman's first rate of pay. After one year of firing turns I received 9s 6d a day. If a cleaner with this rate went back to cleaning engines, as I did, he would still get the fireman's rate. If the cleaners thought their rate of pay low, it is interesting to note that at the same time a conscripted private soldier received just 1/- a day.

Saturday night through to Sunday morning was

usually the time of the week for works trains from Three Bridges. One such night and after the last passenger trains had gone to their destinations, I was rostered with passed fireman Charlie Doyle. What a character! Leaving the up-side yard with a train of materials and a work gang for Redhill Tunnel, we first moved over onto the up slow line, before crossing over to the up fast line. The driver now proceeded to get the train rolling. The green aspects of the electric signals showed up in the dark night and could be seen one after the other for miles ahead – almost as far as the then Gatwick Racecourse station. Charlie suddenly took hold of me in the ballroom dance position and we waltzed around the cab of the 'C2X' to the beat of the exhaust from the chimney! In spite of the dark war years, most drivers remained cheerful and an excellent camaraderie was established. However, black-out sheets were fitted between engine and tender, whilst we also had side sheets. Tank engines just had the side sheets. During the day the sheets were rolled up and tied to the underside of the cab roof whilst the side sheets on tank engines were on rings, so these were drawn back.

One Saturday night I was with another passed fireman, Len Edwards. We had a works train to take to the south end of Clayton Tunnel, the actual Tunnel being 'Under Engineer's Possession'. We were standing just outside the south end of the tunnel, with a 'C2X', while the engineers were working on the up line and on the same side as our works train. My driver said to me "Right lad, take the billycan and fill it with water for a brew up, there is a tap halfway into the tunnel". On my arrival at the halfway mark, surprise, no tap! Men at work there told me the tap was at the mouth of the tunnel – the north end! What a walk that was, all of two and three quarter miles to the water tap and the same distance back to the works train. Whilst this was going on, the down line was still open for single line working and a goods train passed by me on the walk back. The noise from the distant rumble of the goods, deafening when it passed, together with the steam and smoke, had to be heard and seen to be believed in the confines of the tunnel, but it was worth the effort for a cup of tea during a long night. Of course it would have been easier if the can had been filled before we left!

Another incident occurred, although this time on a hot summer's day. I was working on an 'E4' tank, with a passenger train from Horsham to Christ's Hospital and thence over the single line to Guildford. Unfortunately, on this occasion the name of the driver escapes me. I was occupied in firing after which I set the injector and, once satisfied it was singing away glanced over to where the driver was – or should have been! Instead I noticed the reverser in forward gear and regulator open - but no driver! We were traveling at between 40 and 50 miles per hour. All sorts of thoughts

were running through my mind as to what could have happened and what I might do, but before reaching any definite decision I espied him on the engine running plate kneeling down alongside the splasher of the leading wheel. He was evidently peering under the boiler intent on studying the valve gear in motion. How he had managed to walk along what was no more than a very narrow ledge at the base of the tank, holding onto the handrail at the top of the side tank, I could not imagine. There was hardly any foothold and it would have been made more difficult by the swaying of the engine. I never dared to ask him why; perhaps he had heard a knock coming from the engine and if I had asked, he might have expected me to do the same.

Later that same day at Guildford and waiting for our return working, I overheard a passenger talking to a wheel-tapper and enquiring as to his job. The railwayman replied, "I am a wheel-tapper, I tap the wheel and it goes clang". The passenger then asked "What happens when the wheels don't go clang?" The wheel-tapper's reply – "Then I know the train has gone!"

My home in Brighton was in Ditchling Rise which runs parallel to the tall railway viaduct in London Road. Ditchling Rise continues as Argyle Road where, at 12.20 pm on May 25th 1941, a bomb landed and literally bounced in the road. (I remember seeing the groove it left.) It then went through a house and exploded upwards under two arch spans of the railway viaduct, the blast destroying these and leaving the up and down lines to and from Lewes suspended across the now open space. In addition four further bombs dropped the other side of the viaduct, smashing various carriages and trucks, where several railwayman lost their lives. My friend Ken Hillman, who had been a Messenger in London at the same time as me, was now a boiler maker's apprentice in the locomotive works. On hearing the whistling, falling bombs, he dived for cover. Simultaneously, at the school, almost under the arches, on hearing the bombs falling, Ken's mother dashed into the school yard to usher the children there to safety. Sadly Mrs. Hillman died later in hospital. The damaged arches were replaced by a temporary steel structure and it was not long before the trains were running again albeit subject to a severe speed restriction. A permanent repair was affected by October 1941. I recall working on a 'K' class mogul, taking a works train to the viaduct from Three Bridges on one occasion.

Now it was June 1942 and, as an acting fireman one particular morning, I was booked on the 5.20 am goods from East Grinstead to Tunbridge Wells West. After preparing an 'E5' 0-6-0T for the road, I coupled us to a 'C2X' which in turn was coupled to an 'I1X', which was itself finally coupled to an 'I3'. The four engines now crossed the Brighton main line together and headed onto the single line to Rowfant, the single line staff carried, as per the rules, by the last engine. We exchanged 'staffs' in the same way at Rowfant, before continuing on to East Grinstead where we stopped in the platform.

All the engines were now uncoupled, our 'E5' trundling over to the goods yard. Meanwhile the 'I3' continued light to Forest Row, ready to work a London passenger train. The 'I1X' went down the incline to the low level station to work a passenger train to Brighton via Sheffield Park whilst the 'C2X' would work a goods to Oxted. Our own duty was with a goods to Forest Row. Arriving at the station, we passed the 'I3' at the head of its train for London, although our first job was to shunt the yard.

Leaving Forest Row behind us the sun was rising in the east, on my side of the cab. The morning dew was also slowly dispersing, at the start what was a lovely summer's day. The scent from the countryside was like a wonderful perfume that filled the air all around, from the trees, ferns and flowers plus the earth and grass. With only about ten trucks in tow the engine only needed to be lightly worked and I shall always remember the fragrance from the picturesque Sussex countryside on this early morning. Along the way to our next stop at Hartfield and our eventual destination at Tunbridge Wells West, we passed playful hares boxing one another, whilst there was also the occasional glimpse of the colourful plumage of a cock pheasant. The scene, as we trundled along at 25mph, was tranquility itself, and a far cry from the death and destruction occurring not many miles away across the Channel, or indeed the bombing here in England at that time.

After uncoupling in the goods yard at Tunbridge Wells West, it was over to the engine sheds where I cleaned the ash pan and smoke box. Whilst I was doing this my mate was checking the engine for any defects, although just like the morning weather the engine had behaved perfectly. After taking on coal and water it was over to the turntable, finally leaving the engine on one of the shed roads, handbrake screwed hard on, steam cocks open, the steam supply to the Westinghouse pump shut-off and reverser in mid-gear.

Our return working was a passenger train to Three Bridges, for which we often had one of our own engines, 'I1X' No 2600 still at the time in Southern colours. On this occasion, though and for whatever reason, the running foreman gave us sister engine No 2602. But what a difference when we found her; she was painted in allover wartime black which caused my mate to utter, "What a picture of misery!" I agreed; the drab livery of the time did nothing to raise spirits.

Most of the early turns of duty for drivers and firemen at Three Bridges started from 3.00am onwards. As the first stopping train from Brighton to Three Bridges left at 5.48 am, I would instead catch either the 11.15pm van train from Brighton for London Bridge which stopped at Three Bridges, or the 12.40 am Three Bridges goods. This latter service departed from Brighton top yard and was a turn worked by a 'K' class engine, with men from my local depot; indeed, I had been on it as fireman several times. On other occasions, such as when I needed a lift, I would travel with the Guard, often Mr. Chapman, father to an old school chum. The brake van on this service was usually a six-wheeler, known to all as bone-shakers. This was because after passing Clayton Tunnel, the train would get a move on, and the van would start to vibrate and shake the life out of me. How the regular guards put up with such treatment every day I could not imagine.

Not long after the bombing of the viaduct, the family moved to Hove, but still not far from Brighton running sheds. To reach the top yard now I would take a short-cut and walk through the north east corner of the running shed out into the open, over New England Bridge, across some sidings and then finally cross the electrified main line. I was now by the brake van of the 12.40 am goods train. I had gone this way two weeks earlier using the light of the moon to guide me. On this particular black night however, I made the mistake of not having a torch with me. I had crossed the bridge but walked on too far and as I turned to cross the sidings and main line I lifted my foot high over what I thought was the 'juice' rail and stepped over. That is when I fell into a pit full of water. With my fireman's cap on my head I can remember swimming using the breast stroke to the end of the pit, and walking up the steps at the end. I was soaked through to the skin, so I took my well sodden body back to the engine sheds, where there was a sand furnace also used for bringing live coals ready to light up dead engines. In front of the open furnace I undressed and dried out. Fortunately I did not see a soul. When my clothes were reasonably dry, I dressed and took off for the Running Foreman's office. From there I phoned my own Foreman at Three Bridges telling him of my misfortune and why I had missed the goods and was not able to arrive for my rostered firing turn. Of course word soon got around. As I was passing, loco crews would ask each other if they knew who the clown was who took a midnight swim in a pit on his way to work? It took quite a time for me to live that one down. After that ducking I took a longer route to the top yard when going for the goods.

This tale also has a sequel, for, as I found out later, the pits were deliberately kept full of water for use in emergency. Other sheds, such as Nine Elms, kept an old tender or two filled for the same purpose, while there were also some actual fire-trains, with a 'D1' fitted with pumps and hoses ready for use. If only Brighton Shed had used this method instead of a pit filled with

I3s 32028 and 32091 at Tunbridge Wells West on 15ᵗʰ August 1951, 32028 with a train from Three Bridges composed of a SECR 3-coach 'Birdcage' set. The locomotive depot was to the right.

Terry Cole collection.

water I would have stayed dry, although possibly bruised. To be fair, of course, I was also breaking the rules which clearly stated that employees not in the course of their duties, were forbidden to cross the running lines.

Three Bridges running shed did not have any 'D1' tank engines allocated to the shed while I was there, but I did have one trip on a member of the class from Horsham to Brighton. The first part of this turn was an early morning van train from Three Bridges to Bognor, with an 'I3', which we took as far as Horsham. The day was going well; I was with a great mate 'Bungee' Charman and, looking up from my duties near Faygate, I recall seeing his smiling face, lit up by the red glow from the fire-hole half-door opening. Looking in my direction he shouted over "Isn't this great Norm?" If ever a man enjoyed his work on the footplate of an engine, he did.

On arrival at Horsham, a crew from that shed would relieve us and work the train on. 'Bungee' and I waited for a following passenger train from London Bridge, which was routed via West Croydon and Dorking Town and crewed by New Cross Gate men. On this particular day the train rolled in with a 'D1' tank in charge. Changing over with the London crew, we filled the side-tanks and then worked the train to Brighton via

Steyning before working back to Horsham. Usually this would have been with a 'D3' 0-4-4T, although we had also had charge of a 'B4' 4-4-0. Indeed, it seemed the engines that were used for this duty were in their final years or even months before scrapping. Railwayman referred to a trip to Brighton via this route as traveling on the 'linger' - whether this meant it took such a long time to get to our destination or was a cruel indication that the line itself was slowly dying, I am not sure. To be fair, though, an awful lot of lines that closed around the same time were referred to in the same way.

Reverting back to Three Bridges shed again, I recall the occasion when the best efforts of everyone actually made a situation worse. An engine had failed at the station whilst en-route with a vacuum fitted special from Addison Road, Kensington destined for Newhaven. Unfortunately I cannot recall details of the engine that failed, nor the cause and thinking back on it now it was also a bit unusual in that the replacement engine was not taken forward by the same crew. Anyway, I was cleaning engines at the time and together with passed fireman Fred Elliott, we were given orders by Charlie Miller, the Running Foreman, to do a rush job preparing a 'Q' Class 0-6-0 for the road and then to take the train at the station to it's destination. The 'Q' was very light on steam and the water level was also

Left - D3 tank 32378, not on the Steyning line but near Groombridge on a Tunbridge Wells West to Ashurst traon, 13th August 1950.

Opposite - E5 32585 at Tunbridge Wells West 15th August 1951, with a train to Three Bridges. The headcode disc shown is duty No 659, a local turn. The Driver is looking very relaxed as he waits for departure time sitting on the coal bunker top which projected into the cab and formed a very comfortable seat on all the Brighton 'radials'.
Both Terry Cole collection.

low. Fred took the engine to the coal stage where willing hands helped me place a number of large lumps of coal into the firebox. As I was the fireman I should have indicated when to stop, but perhaps through the ignorance of youth I was only too grateful for the well intentioned help.

Unfortunately of course, the coal did not burn through quickly enough, for on the rising incline to Balcombe Signal Box steam pressure had dropped to only 80 psi on the gauge. Fortunately this class was fitted with a powerful ejector to create the vacuum in the train pipe, otherwise the brakes would have automatically been applied. By darting the fire, I had also managed to break up what was a solid mass and when we eventually struggled into the tunnel the worst was over.

Aside from goods and local passenger working, during my time at Three Bridges, the shed also had at least one very important passenger turn which started from Haywards Heath at 3.28pm. To reach it the men rode on the cushions and then took over a local passenger train from a Brighton crew, the usual motive power being either a 'B4X' or 'K' class at the head of four or five coaches having a gross weight of around 200 tons. The destination was London Bridge Terminus (Low Level), reached via Copyhold Junction and Horstead Keynes (the story in my time was that the 'Bluebell Railway' first got its name from the LBSCR gangers who walked the line) and thence to East Grinstead (Low Level) and Oxted. We were ourselves relieved at East Croydon by men from New Cross. Then it was time for another ride on the cushions to Victoria where we then made our way to Platform 15 to relieve a set of Stewarts Land men ready for the 5.50pm

commuter train - fast to East Croydon and then all stations to East Grinstead (High Level). Despite the importance of this train, this time the usual motive power was an old 'I3' tank with just 180 psi boiler pressure, and at times these engines, already long past their best, struggled with the service. Somehow though we always made it but it was invariably with some relief that we were able to shunt the carriages into a siding at our destination. After filling the tanks with water – often almost dry by this time - we returned light to Three Bridges.

Of course, as only a acting fireman at this time, I often reverted to cleaning or shed duties when not required and, as referred to before, this could include being the firelighter, or steam raiser as the job was sometimes called. One night I booked on at 10.00 pm for this duty and as was usual was given a list of engines to attend to by the night foreman, Bert Tyler. All of these were in the actual shed or on adjacent roads. Sometime later something, I don't know what, made me make my way over to the turntable which was a little distance from the shed. I am glad I did as there was an 'N' class hard against the buffer stops. Dead engines were never left here, so out of curiosity I climbed into the cab and, yes, she was in steam, although the fire was almost out and with no water showing in the glass. The injector would also not function. In double quick time I was off to the Foremen's office explaining the problem and that it was not on the list he had given me earlier. We both raced back to the 'N' with a hosepipe, connecting one end to the water main whilst the other end was pushed hard up into the injector overflow pipe. With the water turned on the boiler was back-filled by mains pressure. A close call, but one which saved us the

embarrassment of dropping the lead plugs. I now built up the fire, as the engine was rostered for Battersea Yard later that day. Someone had slipped up, I never found out who as I did not ask, so it was no doubt a cover up. From that time on I always seemed to be in that particular Foreman's good books, even if he did insist on calling me 'Harry', possibly after the popular comedian, Harry Worth. Bert Tyler had a reputation for having been a brilliant engineman and he later became a Locomotive Inspector.

On weekdays Three Bridges men had a regular turn working the Polegate goods service. We would sign on at 9.00 pm, after which there was a walk to the station for another 'on the cushions' ride to Eastbourne. After this came another half mile walk from that station to the shed. During the war years Eastbourne town seemed to be deserted of civilians, although there were plenty of forces personnel around. When we reached the shed we first reported to the Running Foreman who would advise us of our alloted engine, usually an 'N' from Stewarts Lane now working its way back home. After collecting our equipment from the stores we prepared the engine before running light the four miles to Polegate to collect our train. Here I also had to remember to change the headlamps. Backing onto our train, we awaited the right away from the guard and then set off. The destination was our home depot at Three Bridges which was reached sometime after midnight running at an average 30 mph - not bad for a loose coupled service. Indeed the longest time was sometimes waiting at Three Bridges, to set back into the up side yard. We then took the engine to shed and, all being well, I would be ready to catch the 5.00 a.m. newspaper service home to Brighton. I will always remember my driver on these freight trips, Bert Orrin, who without realising it, was a bit of a philosopher. I say this as one night, when I was staring at the steam gauge in disbelief, he simply turned around and commented, "Norman, don't take life so seriously, It's not permanent."

Duties like these made me relish working on larger engines, so when the next vacancy list came up and I saw a vacancy for a fireman at Bournemouth, I jumped at the chance. Fortunately I was successful and was appointed permanent Fireman at Bournemouth at the beginning of September 1943. It would not be long before I was achieving more mileage in a day at my new shed than I had in a week at Three Bridges – but that of course is another story!

I would like to thank Alan Chesterton, Maurice Lee, Ray and Ann Meigan and Ron Stoneman for their help in the compilation of these notes.

Part 2 of Norman's reminiscences covering the time he was based at Bournemouth will feature in a later issue.

VISIT · THE NEWS THEATRE

SOUTHERN

ALL SEASON TICKETS TO BE SHEWN

WATERLOO

LSWR to BR

a brief summary

Kevin Robertson

(Part 2. Part 1 featured in the
September 2007 issue.)

*Left: Journalist Katherine Whitehorn arrives
in London on 3rd March 1956. The picture
was later reproduced in 'Picture Post' under
the heading 'Loneliness in London'.
Katherine Whitehorn remains an active writer
today and has a regular column in 'SAGA'
magazine. Referring to the obvious bustle in
the background, Alan A Jackson in his
scholarly work 'Londons Termini' refers to
Waterloo around this period thus, "Well-
padded widows for Bournemouth avoid sun-
tanned soldiers from Aldershot; Pompey-
bound sailors mix with the luggage-cluttered
cruise passengers that form most of today's
boat train traffic; peachy schoolgirls, up for
the hols from exclusive establishments deep in
Hants, cast sultry glances at red-coated
Chelsea pensioners taking wreaths to a
comrade's funeral. As the rush hours fade,
senior civil servants stride across, black cases
full of last nights drafting; but the City men
avoid the concourse, and are glimpsed only
briefly in their impatient transfer from train to
'Drain'." A 1965 survey also found Waterloo
was the most popular of all the main line
stations for where the homeless might spend
the night, no less than 63 people using the
station faculties or its environs as a temporary
dormitory. On the concourse at Waterloo, for
the benefit of passengers were two sets of
mechanical indicators, situated in front of
platforms 6-7 and 18-19. In addition, a small
enquiry office was placed between Nos 8-9
between the two station bookstalls. Small
hexagonal rotating departure indicators were
provided on those platforms used by electric
trains, 1 through to 6, and 16 through to 21.
Iron railings of the type seen, together with
platform tickets were introduced from 7th May
1913 whilst automatic machines for the issue
of such tickets were in use, certainly by 1918.*

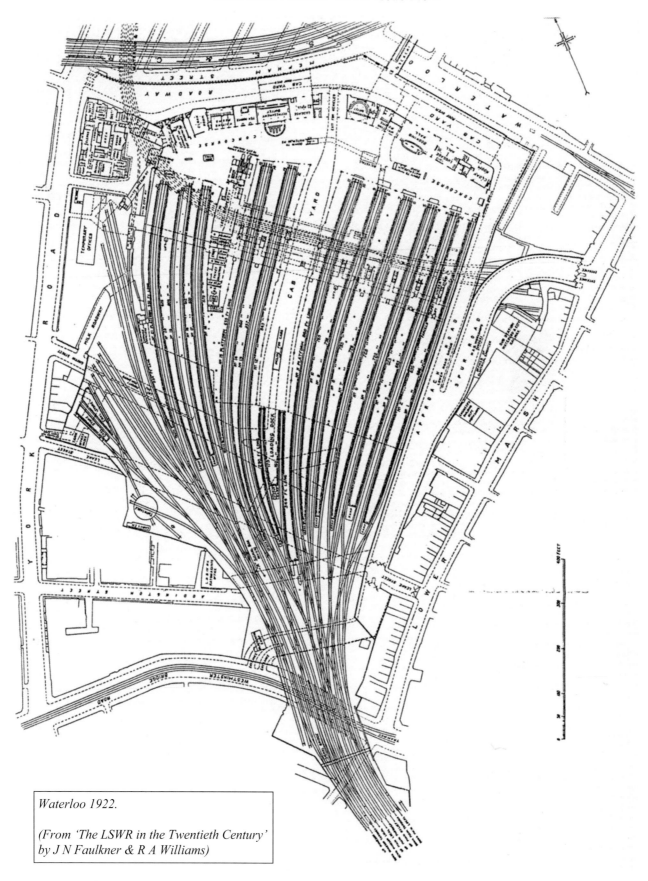

Waterloo 1922.

*(From 'The LSWR in the Twentieth Century'
by J N Faulkner & R A Williams)*

Again the records for new work around this period are slightly confusing, as there is a reference to the new 'Windsor Tea-Room' which opened in July 1921. (But what happened to the facility operated by the firm of Spiers & Pond and spoken of in 1913?) [1] Indeed a later, 1922 report, contemporaneous with the formal opening, referred to the kitchens being placed above the concourse level dining room and, likewise, also above the first floor oak-panelled 'Surrey' dining room and Ladies' tea-room. This was planned so that diners would not be offended by cooking smells. Remaining on the subject of refreshments, there was also a "large buffet behind the ticket office" brought into use on 23rd December 1921, "...which replaced the temporary refreshment rooms in use since July 1916." (Presumably though, not the same as those for the soldiers.)

The final instruction on the rebuilding was given on 20th December 1919, with directions for the archway leading into the station opposite Platforms 19 and 20 to be completed as the Company War Memorial to the 585 LSWR employees who lost their lives. It would also become known as The Victory Arch.

Completed, the station was finally ready for a formal opening in 1922 and it was anticipated that this would be undertaken by The King and Queen. Accordingly on 21st March 1922 Queen Mary arrived alone – King George V was 'indisposed' with a chill. Her Majesty arrived at the roadway and the usual presentations were made. After this she cut a blue ribbon across 'The Victory Arch' before making what was referred to as 'a brief tour of the concourse', prior to driving back to Buckingham Palace. For the next week the Victory – or Memorial Arch, as it was also referred to - was floodlit. (King George V subsequently visited the station, for travel purposes, on 5th August 1922.)

Quite understandably the LSWR, in what was also its last year of existence, was keen to extol the virtues of the new station and a 24 page section in the April 1922 issue (Volume V111, No 85) of the 'South Western Railway Magazine' was devoted entirely to the station – this was subsequently reprinted as a separate publication and also contains a number of useful photographs.

Some commentators went so far as to compare the architecture of the Victory Arch with that of classical Italian, whilst perhaps a more pertinent comment was that "...the old Waterloo Station was a by-word for confusion, the new station may be

Above: No. 776 'Sir Galagars', left, and an unidentified 2-6-0 await departure for the West of England and Southampton respectively. Just visible on the right is a 'Paddlebox'. The 2-6-0 is a 'U' rebuilt from a 'K' class 2-6-4T and is on a boat train to Millbrook (West) Docks.

Dave Hammersley collection

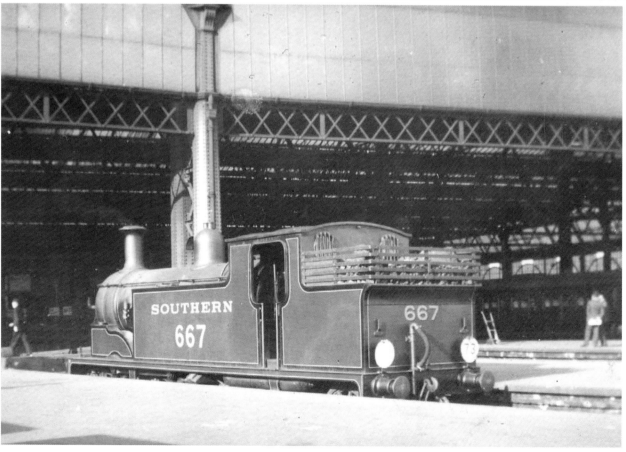

'WATERLOO SNAPS'

- the going -

Opposite - upper: 'M7' No 125 (?) possibly ready to depart with milk for the West London line. These platforms were also originally used for vehicles used for transporting private carriages and were officially loading-docks. Although officially reported as having 21 public platforms, there were in fact 26 platform faces. These included the double faces seen on the short platforms here and also a further bay on the far side of No 21. The longest platform was No 11, at 860 feet.

Opposite - lower: Another 'M7', No 667 In pristine livery and about to leave light for Nine Elms or Clapham.

This page - top: No E475 reported as in charge of the 6.00 pm Plymouth express.

This page - centre: Recorded sometime before withdrawal in September 1931, Adams 'X2' No 585 is recorded at Waterloo on what is either a local or a Southampton service.

This page - lower: Another veteran, but this time which would last in service until November 1935. 'C8' 4-4-0 No 296. At this stage the engine was based at Salisbury and would normally have been employed on local services from that shed. Its appearance at Waterloo then could well have been due to extra traffic requirements.

All Dave Hammersley collection

'WATERLOO SNAPS' - and the coming -

considered as one for ordered simplicity."

The new Waterloo was the final major engineering work undertaken by LSWR. But bear in mind that concurrent with the expenditure on the station, the LSWR had also undertaken a number of other major works since 1900. These included the Southampton Docks, widening of the main line, suburban electrification, the new Locomotive Works at Eastleigh and a host of new lines including the Meon Valley route. Even so it was still able to pay a dividend in the order of 6% throughout. (For a financial summary, the reader is referred to Appendix 13 on Page 216 of "Faulkner & Williams".)

For many years the concourse boasted a full size relic of early times, in the shape of an original Bodmin & Wadebridge Railway coach, located on rails set in granite blocks and opposite Platform 9. Years later when the station was under threat of bombing in WW2, the staff were well aware of its historic significance and it was moved to the shelter of the arches beneath the station. These same arches also found themselves used as bomb shelters for the populace in both wars and which could accommodate up to 6,500 persons as well as emergency offices for the railway.

Above: N15X, 2331 'Beattie' and Schools, No 932 'Blundells', sometime between April and October 1936.

Opposite page - upper: Reported as an Ocean liner Express arriving, in charge of 'H15' class No. 521.

Opposite page - lower: 'Waterloo in Ascot Week'. 'H16' No 517 having no doubt brought in empty stock. Certainly for the greater part of its era as a steam terminus, the station was noted for both its movement of men destined for the armed forces and, at more relaxing times, when race goers flocked for trains. In the former category would be men destined for Southampton as a point of embarkation as well as the Aldershot, Bordon and Salisbury as well as the equivalent naval traffic for Portsmouth, Portland and Plymouth – Devonport. Race goers would travel to Epsom, Windsor, Sandown Park, Hurst Park, Ascot, Kempton Park and Salisbury. Perhaps as many as 14,000 punters alone were transported to one meeting in the 1950s, necessitating any number of special trains. In earlier years, particularly the 1900s, it was reported that there were five daily horse box services from the terminus.

All Dave Hammersley collection

WATERLOO STATION
CHRONOLOGY OF RECONSTRUCTION

Old Station				New Station	
Platform Road	Renumbered 1/10/12,7/12/13		Out of use	Platform	Into use
				1	24/1/09
				2	24/1/09
(South Station)				3	24/1/09
1			24/1/09	4	25/7/09
2			24/1/09	5	6/3/10
Cab road and approach				5A/6	9/3/13
Station offices				6/7	29/6/13
(Central Station)				6A/8	20/7/13
1	3	6	29/6/13	9	21/12/13
2	4		3/7/11	10	21/12/13
–	5	Middle road removed 1902 (5 from 1902)	3/7/11	11	7/12/13
3 {	6				
	7 }	7	1/10/13	Cab roadway	
4	7			Dock sidings	8/14
Dock 8		8 Siding	8/14		
(Windsor Extension)					
5	9	9 12	25/4/15	12	20/8/16
6 {	10	10 13	25/4/15	13	27/8/16
	11	11 14	25/4/15	14	29/10/16
7	12	12 15	25/4/15	15	30/5/17
(North Station)					
7	13	13 16	Reconstructed	16	13/6/15
8 {	14	14 17	Reconstructed	17	11/4/15
	15	15 18	Reconstructed	18	11/4/15
9 {	16	16 19	Reconstructed	19	14/6/14
	17	17 20	Reconstructed	20	14/2/15
10	18	Milk Milk	Reconstructed	21	28/2/15

Notes: Platforms 5A, 6 and 6A were renumbered 6, 7 and 8 respectively from 1/10/13. After being taken out of public use platform lines sometimes remained as sidings, and new lines were formed as sidings while platforms were being constructed.

Above: N15X, No 2327 'Trevithick' awaiting departure for Salisbury probably post-war judging by the malachite livery with green deflectors.

HMRS collection AB7008 (V1179)

Left: From 'The LSWR in the Twentieth Century' by J N Faulkner & R A Williams.

Opposite page - top: Taken from the cab of 10202 entering the terminus at 11.05 am sometime in July 1952. Left to right 34011 'Tavistock' is at the head of Southampton Docks Boat train, 30478 is waiting to take empty coaching stock, and 34009 'Lyme Regis' is in charge of the 11.30 Bournemouth West service.

Arthur Tayler

Loudspeaker announcements were first provided from 9th March 1932, although just less than ten years earlier the first signs of commercialism appeared with the opening of a branch of the National Provincial Bank on the concourse. Later, of course, the venue would be the site for a veritable explosion in retail outlets.

I would like to thank Rod Garner, Reg Randall, Dennis Tillman and Colin Chivers for their help and encouragement in the preparation of these notes.
Several standard reference works no doubt familiar to most readers have been consulted, including;

London's Termini, by Alan A Jackson, The London & South Western Railway, by O S Nock. The London & South Western Railway, by Hamilton Ellis. The LSWR in the Twentieth Century, by J N Faulkner & R A Williams. Sir Herbert Walker's Southern Railway, by C F Clapper. The Southern Railway, by C F Dendy Marshall - revised edition. The South Western Gazzette. The Southern Magazine.

(1.) Christopher Pond (1826-1881) hailed from Essex and met Londoner Felix Spiers (1832-1910) in Australia at the time of the gold rush in 1851. They rented a room at the Melbourne National Hotel, set it up as a catering establishment and named it 'The Shakespeare Grill Room'. Later they bought the Café de Paris in Melbourne and made a fortune, both from this and providing catering on the Melbourne-Ballarat Railway. They organised the visit of the first English cricket team to Australia in 1861/2. They also organized the first balloon flight in Australia.
Spiers & Pond later returned to England and introduced railway catering to the UK on the Metropolitan Railway and the London, Chatham & Dover Railway. They built the Criterion Restaurant and Theatre, Piccadilly Circus (1874), the Gaiety Theatre Restaurant in the Strand (1894) and they catered at the Regents Park Zoo and at the Theatre Royal, Drury Lane. They also produced an 80 page monthly mail order catalogue, The Housekeeper, which provided articles of interest, recipes and hints to housewives.

Waterloo, recorded on 2nd June 1954. The 1936 signalbox is seen here as well as its associated electric signals all operated by miniature levers. Despite the lack of trains we do not believe there was any industrial action taking place at this time, just a rather quite time mid-week.

THE GETTY FILES No 1

Passengers boarding a Weymouth bound service on 26th May 1950, the Friday of the bank holiday. Beneath the station and running the complete width of the station - until the Eurostar rebuilding, was the famous Waterloo Plan Arch, where the equally renowned Reg Randall was in charge for many years. Numerous researchers including the present writer, owe much to Reg and his compatriots. The length of the train will be noted, indeed from the operators perspective a 12-coach train with an engine at either end could be at headache, as only Nos 11 through to 14 could deal with such stock and that was after they had been extended.

Worth mentioning is the 1961 film 'Terminus' by John Schlesinger, produced by British Transport Films, which depicts 24 hours in the life of the station.

51

Hulton Archive / Getty Images 3066539

Above and lower right: 19th June 1947 and Nine Elms based 'Battle of Britain', 21C161 is recorded at Weybridge with the 8-coach Ilfracombe portion of the "Devon Belle". This was a special circular press trip, from Waterloo and back to Waterloo, via Byfleet, Virginia Water and Staines. The public service commenced the following day, Friday 20th June. From the lower view it can be seen that the observation car was clearly popular.

S C Townroe / R K Blencowe collection

Left: One of just three contemporary books produced on famous trains of the period. (The others were the 'Flying Scotsman' and the 'Royal Scot'.) The book was similar to the various "...through the window.....titles" and included a route map of the various stages of the journey, complete with drawings of relevant points of interest. The engine depicted on the front cover was shown in blue livery.

FOR WHOM THE BELLE TOLLS...

***Jeffery Grayer** recalls the brief heyday and rapid decline of the Southern's prestigious 'Devon Belle', which was to run for just eight seasons.*

Passengers who took their seats aboard a gleaming rake of Pullman cars drawn up at Waterloo on 20th June 1947 were startled to hear a disembodied voice seemingly coming from the ether, but in reality emanating from speakers hidden in the coach ceilings, announcing "*Ladies and gentlemen this is the 'Devon Belle' calling…..*" The coaching stock for this prestigious new service, introduced by the Southern Railway a few months before nationalisation, housed one of the first public address systems to be installed on a British railway. Further amazement to passengers was no doubt caused when an actor, posing as Sir Francis Drake resplendent in Elizabethan costume, took his seat on the inaugural train with the intention of joining the civic reception at Plymouth. But, as was the custom with new services, special cocktails christened the "Spirit of Drake" and the ""Devon Belle" Cup" were served on the train. Whether this had anything to do with the fact that the actor was still sitting in the Observation Car at Exeter Central, after the Plymouth portion had departed is not recorded ! However, a rapid car journey from Exeter ensued, just managing to beat the train into Plymouth, and Sir Francis was able to join in the reception as planned.

The all-Pullman 'Devon Belle' set a new standard of comfort and luxury for the journey west to Exeter, Ilfracombe and Plymouth. It also had a unique feature, an Observation Car nick-named "The Glasshouse", which brought up the rear of the Ilfracombe portion and which featured heavily on the advertising material for the service. Upon arrival at Ilfracombe, this car had to be removed from the rear of the down train, turned on the turntable and repositioned at the rear of the following day's Belle. A similar procedure applied at Waterloo where, after the empty coaching stock had been drawn out to Clapham Yard, the Observation Car was detached and taken back to Waterloo, usually by an M7, where it was turned on the table at the terminus. One could usually see this performance just after 9 pm in the evenings when the train ran. After turning it was trundled back to Clapham and restored to the coaching set.

The inaugural down train was hauled by Merchant Navy class 21C15, "Rotterdam Lloyd", then just over two years old, from Waterloo to Wilton where the locomotive was changed for another Merchant Navy, 21C3, "Royal Mail". This took the service onwards to Exeter where Light Pacifics took over their respective portions for Plymouth and Ilfracombe. Appropriately enough the inaugural up and down trains, from Plymouth and Ilfracombe, were hauled west of Exeter Central by their namesake West Country class locomotives 21C103 "Plymouth" and 21C117 "Ilfracombe".

Two Pullman observation cars were in traffic for the up and down services, numbered 13 and 14, but they were not new-builds having started life in other guises. N°14 was built in 1918 originally as an LNWR Ambulance car and converted into a Pullman car in 1921. It was rebuilt as a Bar car in 1937, and finally remodelled as an Observation Car, the conversion taking place at the Pullman Company's Preston Park works in Brighton during 1947. The single and double "cup" seats in these cars were purposefully made somewhat

The July 1947 'Southern Railway Magazine' carried a three page article on the new train - part of which is also reproduced overleaf. The accompanying photograph carried an amount of journalistic licence, as although stated as being, "The first (down) 'Devon Belle' hauled by a 'West Country' class locomotive, No 21C161 passing Weybridge". This was, of course, the previous day's press outing.

According to the SOUTHERN RAILWAY MAGAZINE "Drake arrived West! The Lord Mayor of Plymouth assists Sir Francis to alight." Again, of course, journalistic licence, clearly "Sir Francis" would not have travelled all the way on the front buffer but, as also described in the text, he actually completed the last 60 miles by road and not even in the train!

SOUTHERN RAILWAY MAGAZINE
Vol XXV No 268 July 1947

"….Many comments were heard remarking on the Southern Railway's enterprise in difficult times, with tributes to the Pullman Car Company for the 'truly-Pullman' service, and to Messrs Lyons who had supplied from Cadby Hall the first 'Frood' meal to be eaten on a train. This 'Frood' (or Frozen Food) is the product of a waste-eliminating service of supplying food prepared long beforehand, the result being a superb hot meal of high-class restaurant standard.

"For the send off from Waterloo on June 20, the Chairman of the SR, Colonel Eric Gore Browne, was present, with the General manager, Sir Eustace Missenden, and Mr S J Adams, Chairman and Managing Director of the Pullman Car Co., together with important officials. As extremely picturesque figure on the platform was 'Sir Francis Drake' (Eric Gillingham), whose pointed head and Elizabethan raiment fitted the occasion. Short speeches were made, photographs were taken and filming was carried on. 'Drake' then made a courtly bow, took his place in the train and proceeded to 'Go West', and the 'Devon Belle' steamed out amid enthusiasm, so adding another picturesque episode in railway history.

"Punctually at 3.36 pm the 'Devon Belle' arrived at Exeter Central Station. The SR Band played on the platform. The train was welcomed by the Deputy Mayor (Mr G J Greenslade) who was accompanied by the Sherriff (Mr C W H Hill). It remained in the station for ten minutes before continuing its journey in two sections - one to Barnstaple and Ilfracombe, the other to Plymouth.

"At 5.32 pm the Ilfracombe portion arrived at the North Devon resort. On the platform were Mr E G Baugh, Chairman of the Ilfracombe Council, members of the local authority , and representatives of the North Devon Water Board and Ilfracombe Chamber of Trade. The Ilfracombe train was hauled by 'West Country' class locomotive No 21C117 'Ilfracombe', and the engine was driven by Mr Herbert Jones, a local man.

"At Plymouth the 'Devon Belle' was welcomed by the Lord Mayor (Mr Harry Taylor) at Friary Station. There was a roll of drums by the Royal Marine Cadets Band as the Lord Mayor shook hands with the engine driver, Mr W E Snell. A further roll greeted Eric Gillingham as, dressed as Sir Francis Drake, he leapt from the train.

"Fireman W Symonds, and Guard E Yandall (the latter at 73, is the oldest guard in Plymouth) also shook hands with the Lord Mayor.

"Friary Station was decorated with flags and the Lord Mayor, who was welcomed by Mr P Hayman, Stationmaster, was presented with a photograph of the train."

21C5 'Canadian Pacific' at the head of the full train about to leave Exeter Central on the second day of service, Saturday 21ˢᵗ June 1947.

On the first day of working, 21C15 took the train from Waterloo to Wilton (Nine Elms Duty No 6) and 21C3 from thence to Exeter. 21C4 was used for the return run between Exeter and Wilton.

The two portions of the up 'Devon Belle' at Exeter Central on the second day of the full service, Saturday 21ˢᵗ June 1947.
Right is the Ilfracombe portion, appropriately hauled by 21C117, whilst below is the Plymouth section, again appropriately hauled by 21C103. Both engines had worked the same turns on the inaugural day and were specially prepared at Exmouth Junction beforehand.

Dep		Dep
12.00	Waterloo	17.20 arr
15.16	Sidmouth Junc	14.03
15.36	Exeter Ctrl	13.40
17.16	Devonport	11.47
17.36	Plymouth Fry.	11.30
16.49	B'staple Junc	12.37
16.55	B'staple Town	12.32
17.05	Braunton	12.23
17.23	Mortehoe	12.12
17.32 arr	Ilfracombe	12.00

PS ($\frac{5}{40}$)

SOUTHERN RAILWAY

INSTRUCTION
No. 3 a, 1947.

Special instructions to all concerned as to the exchange of engines on the "Devon Belle" passenger trains at WILTON.

To operate on and from Friday, 20th June, 1947.

The following instructions must be observed by all concerned in connection with the exchange of engines on the "Devon Belle" passenger trains at WILTON :—

The engine which is to work the down train forward must be berthed in the down siding and that which is to work the up train forward must be berthed in the up sidings preparatory to the arrival of the relevant train and thereafter the procedure must be as shown below :—

DOWN TRAIN.

(a) When the down train has come to a stand at the platform, the engine must be detached and, provided the down starting signal has been placed to the "off" position, must proceed to the Dinton side of the West crossover road points where it must be brought to a stand at the shunting signal controlling movements back over those points.

(b) The engine which is to work the train forward, must be accompanied by a Shunter, who must warn the Driver of the occupation of the line ahead by the engine referred to in paragraph (a), and then be shunted from the down siding to the down line and brought to a stand at the shunting signal controlling movements back over the down siding points. When the down siding points have been restored to their normal position and the shunting signal has been lowered this engine must set back on and be coupled to the train standing at the down platform.

(c) The detached train engine referred to in paragraph (a) must then, provided the shunting signal at which it is standing has been placed to the "off" position, proceed to the up line, or to the down siding provided the shunting signal at the down siding points ahead has also been lowered.

UP TRAIN.

(d) When the up train has come to a stand at the platform the engine must be detached and, provided the up starting signal has been placed to the "off" position, must proceed to the Salisbury side of the up siding points where it must be brought to a stand at the shunting signal controlling movements back over those points. When the up siding points have been reversed and the shunting signal has been lowered the engine must proceed to the up sidings.

(e) The engine which is to work the train forward must be accompanied by a Shunter and then be shunted from the up sidings to the up line and brought to a stand at the shunting signal controlling movements back over the up siding points. When the up siding points have been restored to their normal position and the shunting signals applicable to the movement have been placed to the "off" position, this engine must proceed and be coupled to the train standing at the up platform.

(f) All engine movements must be supervised by a competent Shunter who must make use of the return bell communication with the signal box in accordance with the prescribed codes and the Signalman must be careful to ensure that points and shunting signals are operated strictly in accordance with the bell codes received from the Shunter.

MOVEMENTS ON TO RUNNING LINES ALREADY OCCUPIED.

Exception 2—Movements authorised when line ahead occupied by a train or vehicles not conveying passengers.

The following to be added to the list of places under the above heading on page 163 of the Western Appendix to the Working Time Tables :—

Place	Authorised movement	Remarks
WILTON	Light engine shunting from down siding to down line preparatory to setting back to train at down platform.	Shunter must accompany movement and warn Driver of occupation of line ahead.

WATERLOO STATION.
2nd June, 1947.   (R. 73,495).

S. W. SMART,
Superintendent of Operation.

Wilton, just west of Salisbury and the down train paused at the platform in consequence of the engine changing operation.

In 1947 a new 70' turntable was installed at Exmouth Junction, which was partly due to the proposal to built an 8,000 gallon tender. This would then have allowed non-stop working between Waterloo and Exeter.

The locomotive seen is 35004, waiting to take over the down working on 14th May 1948. Actual engine changing was scheduled to take six minutes.

Both: R K Blencowe collection

Opposite page: Courtesy Yeovil Railway Centre

less comfortable than usual, to encourage a rapid changeover of clientele! After the "'Devon Belle'" service ended in 1954, the Observation Cars were used on charter services before ending up in maroon livery on the Scottish Region in 1961. Here they worked the routes from Inverness to the Kyle of Lochalsh and from Glasgow to Oban. After withdrawal in 1967, Car 14 went to North America as part of the 'Flying Scotsman' tour train of 1969. Travelling extensively around the USA and Canada, the vehicle was exhibited with the train at the 1970 Toronto exhibition before ending up in San Francisco where it remained after the locomotive was returned to the UK. It stayed there until recently,

being successfully repatriated following an appeal. It arrived at Southampton Docks on 26th February 2007 and will probably be restored at Derby before entering service on the Swanage Railway. The other Observation Car, No 13, does duty in this capacity on the preserved Paignton and Dartmouth Railway.

The distinctive wing nameplates of this train, which were attached to the locomotive smoke deflectors, had a red background colour with cream lettering, a departure from the normal green background used on Southern headboards. A headboard in similar colours was also carried on top of the buffer beam. In 1953 the wing plates were dispensed with and the now redundant

21C103 on the down Plymouth working near Sampford Courteney on 29th August 1947. It would appear 21C103 and 21C117 were regular performers on the respective portions west of Exeter for some time during the first summer. One exception was on 4th July when 21C145 was substituted for the former and was only able to display the front headboard as the smoke deflectors had not been drilled as required. More serious was the delay occasioned on the following day, when the down workings were 78 minutes late leaving Exeter due to the main train having been derailed at catch-points following the need to set back after a signal check at Sutton Bingham near Yeovil Junction. On this occasion the Ilfracombe portion consisted of just four Pullmans and two ordinary corridor coaches.
The lower view is of 21C105 being banked by 21C102 between Ilfracombe and Mortehoe.

Both: R K Blencowe collection

fixing battens were removed from the smoke deflectors. A new style SR pattern headboard, fixed to the smokebox door, was also now carried.

The idea for the 'Devon Belle' was actually not the Southern's but emanated from the Pullman Car Company, who put a proposal for the all Pullman service to Waterloo in 1946. Pullman had spare cars it was anxious to get back into revenue earning service to offset lack of trade during the war. The SR had lost some 450 coaches during the conflict, so it was felt that using Pullmans might go some to way to addressing this shortfall. Petrol continued to be rationed so the motorist, who tended at this stage, before the age of mass motoring to be from the wealthier sections of society,

had every incentive to leave their car at home and travel by rail. Sir Eustace Missenden, Chairman of the SR, was a great supporter of Pullman and in his speech given at the launch of the new Belle service spoke of "*A gracious lady in our midst*". A special press run took place on 19th June when 21C161 had performed the honours trundling journalists around the Surrey countryside.

Say '"Devon Belle"' to any railway enthusiast and nine times out of ten the first thing that comes to mind is the seemingly bizarre Wilton engine change – some extra information on which may not also go amiss. Historically all passenger trains had been obliged to stop at Salisbury since the 1904 accident, but in their wisdom

Banking the up Ilfracombe portion between the two stations at Exeter and about to enter Queen Street Tunnel. The engine is E1/R No 2695. (An article on this class of engine working in the West Country was featured in Southern Way No 1.) M Whitehouse collection

the SR decided perversely to stop at Wilton, 2½ miles further west instead. This was surely just a publicity gimmick for not only did it miss the traffic potential to be gained by serving the cathedral city but it required unnecessary light engine movements between Wilton and Salisbury shed. The stated intention was, that as it had been decided not to cater for Salisbury, it was preferable not to occupy a platform there to change engines whilst the lack of water troughs on the Southern demanded a stop on the London – West of England run, somewhere in the vicinity of Salisbury, to take water or change engines. At Wilton, as at Exeter Central, a porter was charged with the task of going to the rear of the Observation Car with a short ladder, a bucket of water and a leather and cleaning the rear windows, to ensure the view remained as clear as possible, in the standard time allowance of five minutes or so permitted for engine changing. After returning to Salisbury shed for servicing and turning the locomotive relieved from the down service would head the up "Devon Belle" later in the day. From 6th February 1950, with improved maintenance and the more widespread availability of Bulleid Pacifics, through engine workings were instituted for other passenger services between Waterloo and Exeter although of necessity with a water stop at

Salisbury. Even so the Belle stubbornly continued to change locomotives at Wilton. It was estimated that the new arrangements applicable to other services witnessed some 27 less engine changes at Salisbury and seven at Exeter Central. Consideration was even given to the introduction of 8,000 gallon tenders so that locomotives could work through to Exeter without stopping for water but the idea was not pursued. Thus the Belle continued to creep through Salisbury at 15 mph, a special banner signal on the down centre road at the eastern end of the platform having been installed to control this movement. It was not to be until the last year of operation that common sense prevailed and a stop at Salisbury was finally inserted into the schedule.

The standard formation was four cars for Plymouth and eight, including the Observation Car, for Ilfracombe. At times of peak demand fourteen vehicles, with a tare load topping 540 tons (575 tons with passengers and luggage) and sometimes even up to sixteen Pullmans, was not unknown. The main problem was of course that these seasonal peaks were very short. Dragging the Belle's considerable weight up and down the Devon banks of the LSWR switchback mainline from Salisbury meant that the 83 minute schedule for the 73.3 miles between Wilton and Sidmouth Junction,

London bound from Devon, the up train shortly after leaving Sidmouth Junction

the first booked stop, was quite demanding even for a brand new Bulleid Pacific. Additionally, west of Exeter with such a heavy train banking assistance between Braunton and Mortehoe on the down service and from a standing start up the 1 in 36 at Ilfracombe on the Waterloo leg was of course required and often two bankers and one locomotive ahead of the train engine was the order of the day at Exeter St Davids for the up services.

One big attraction, when the Belle was first introduced, was the availability of reserved seats, something that was not possible at that time, even on the "Atlantic Coast Express" nor on any of the competing services from Paddington. Unfortunately this advantage did not last long for seat reservations were generally re-introduced in 1948 for weekday services and in 1949 for weekend workings. The normal single fare in 1947 from Ilfracombe to London was £2 18s 11d First Class, and £1 15s 4d Third Class. Additionally these attracted Pullman supplements of 8/4d and 4/6d respectively.

An unusual perspective taken 'somewhere west of Exeter' (any ideas as to the exact location would be welcome.) It has been suggested that after arrival of the complete train at Waterloo the initial arrangement was for the complete 500 ton rake to be turned by being hauled by an M7 on a circular route from Clapham Junction to Teddington, Twickenham, Richmond and back to Clapham. Later the simpler method as described in the text was adopted.
S C Townroe / R K Blencowe collection

In mixed Southern and BR identity, 35010 is recorded at what is believed to be Salisbury. The headboard carried is of the original type and may be compared with that seen on the next page.

R K Blencowe collection

In the standard formation of eight cars for Ilfracombe, seats were provided for 68 First Class and 138 Third Class passengers. A further 27 seats were available in what was the 'classless' Observation Car although these could not be booked ahead. The Plymouth portion had 124 seats, 102 of which were Third Class. A kitchen was provided for every two cars and, of course, full Pullman catering was provided at every seat. No less than 22 Pullman staff were employed on the train and, so that they could spend a comfortable night at each terminus, old Pullman cars had been especially equipped at both Plymouth and Ilfracombe. Another innovation was the sale of books and periodicals on the move, whilst during the journey an attendant came through the train with a specially designed portable bookstall. This service was inaugurated to celebrate the 100th birthday of the well known booksellers W H Smith & Son on 30th August 1948. At the forward end of the Observation Car was a curved recess containing a mural map of the route to Devon, designed by Eleanor Esmonde-White, and behind this was a small buffet and toilet. The labour intensive nature of the working was increased with the use of no less than nine men in London from 06.00 on the morning of each departure, cleaning and polishing the cars ready for use.

For the first year, 1947, the train operated on Fridays, Saturdays, Sundays and Mondays until 27th October. This initial season was not without incident. On 22nd September as the up Belle was passing the down ACE between Honiton and Sidmouth Junction one of the Belle's wingplates became detached from the smoke deflectors of the locomotive and proceeded to ricochet between the coaching sets of the two expresses both of which were touching 60mph. In the resultant mayhem the windows and bodies of the first two Pullmans were damaged, together with no less than seven coaches of the ACE. Seven passengers were injured by flying glass. The two Pullmans were detached at Wilton and the damaged ACE coaches at Exeter Central with consequent 45 minute delays to both services.

The 1948 season ran from 14th May – 26th October, with the addition of a down train on Thursdays and a balancing up train on Tuesdays, leaving Wednesday as the only day without a service. In 1949, for example, the down service left Waterloo at noon arriving at Ilfracombe at 17.33 and Plymouth at 17.36. Up services left Plymouth at 11.30 and Ilfracombe at noon arriving into Waterloo at 17.20. After Exeter Central the Plymouth portion, which because of the Observation Car at the rear of the train was always

35015 near Wilton with the down train on 24th July 1954 and the last leg of the working for the engine from Waterloo. On this occasion the train is made up of 13 bogie vehicles. This was the same engine that had hauled the first down train in 1947 and although not confirmed as such, it is likely that the majority of the workings between Waterloo and Exeter were in the hands of 'Merchant Navy' class engines.

Train	Formation	Summer 1947	
Ilfracombe Portion			
Train 1	**Train 2**	**Seats**	**Vehicle Type**
Minerva	Princess Elizabeth	24	1st Parlour
Cynthia	Rosamund	22	1st Kitchen
Fingall	Geraldine	22	1st Kitchen
No 35	No 34	42	3rd Parlour
No 169	No 249	30	3rd Kitchen
No 60	No 32	36	3rd Kitchen
No 65	No 27	30	3rd Brake
No 14	No 13	27	Observation
Plymouth Portion			
No 36	No 208	36	3rd Parlour
Ilolanthe	Argus	22	1st Kitchen
No 61	No 33	36	3rd Kitchen
No 55	No 54	30	3rd Brake

marshalled first in the rake, called only at Exeter St Davids, Okehampton, Tavistock (from 1948), Devonport and Plymouth. Although reports often spoke of "14 well-filled Pullman coaches" in the first year or two of operation in truth the Belle's initial impact began to fade as early as 1949 when that summer's revenue failed to meet operating costs. As patronage had never been as great on the Plymouth route it was decided to terminate this portion at Exeter for the 1950 season. The cutting out of the Plymouth portion resulted in a six minute reduction in overall journey time to Ilfracombe. In the summer of 1950 the unbalanced Thursday and Tuesday workings were also withdrawn.

These reductions freed up the carriage sets which were used to earn some additional revenue, in a series of Wednesday tourist rail-tours to popular destinations, run in conjunction with Messrs. Thomas Cook. On 9th August 1950, for example, an excursion ran from Victoria to Canterbury Cathedral or Dover, and on 22nd August one operated from Waterloo to Yeovil, for Wells Cathedral by road. The following year on 8th August a special from Victoria ran to

Chichester, for the Cathedral, or for a cruise on Southampton Water and on 20th August 1952 a Waterloo – Dorchester excursion was worked consisting of seven Pullmans plus the Observation Car.

In February 1952 withdrawal of the service, after just five seasons' operation, was announced but remarkably the decision was rescinded just a week later, the Exeter "Express & Echo" carried an obituary for the service in March which proved to be somewhat premature. Even so 1952's operations were further limited to a down train on Fridays, both up and down workings on Saturdays and Sundays and an up train on Mondays. In 1953 and 1954 a similar pattern was observed. However, in 1954 an abortive attempt to boost revenue on a Friday was tried by despatching the train in the late afternoon at 16.40, dropping the Wilton stop and finally adopting a publicly advertised stop at Salisbury, also inserting a further stop at Axminster. Consequently Ilfracombe was not reached until 21.48. Often the load by this date, even in August, was no more than five cars plus the Observation saloon. This was to remain the pattern until what were to prove to be the final runs, down on Saturday 15th September and up the following day. Although no public announcement was made, the death knell for the "Devon Belle" had sounded and the train did not appear in the 1955 schedules.

As a replacement, from 1955 onwards, a noon, or thereabouts, departure from Ilfracombe ran to timings similar to the Belle but without of course the luxury of Pullman cars, arriving at Waterloo 5 minutes earlier than the Belle. The 12.05 Waterloo – Ilfracombe restaurant car service filled the gap on summer Saturdays, reaching Ilfracombe at 17.33. This train did not have a Plymouth portion but did shed coaches at Barnstaple Junction bound for Torrington.

Although lasting for only a few seasons, the "Devon Belle", which could never be classified a financial success, was, however, never in the same league as the GWR's ill fated "Torquay Pullman" which embarrassingly lasted for only one summer, in 1929, before being rapidly withdrawn.

There were a number of reasons for the failure of the "Devon Belle", perhaps the most crucial being the limited number of days on which the train operated together with its seasonal nature. This meant that, even had it run fully loaded, it is doubtful whether it would have been financially successful, given that the utilisation of its stock and staff were so poor. In truth the service did not provide any significant benefit over the more established "Atlantic Coast Express", which left Waterloo an hour earlier and reached Ilfracombe in pretty much the same overall running time. One could also dine in the more conventional train, admittedly in somewhat plainer surroundings, without the penalty of the Pullman supplement, though of course the attraction of the Observation Car was lacking. In truth, the destinations which the "Devon Belle" served did not have the wealthy business and commuter clientele which the SR's other more successful Pullmans had in Brighton, Bournemouth and Dover.

The down working near Dinton and with just nine vehicles in tow including the observation car. By this time, 27th August 1954, the train had less than three weeks running left whilst it will be noted also that from 1952 under BR days the smokebox wing plates were discarded and the then standard type of headboard was fitted.

E W Fry / R K Blencowe collection

The South Eastern and Chatham Railway loved coaches with saloons, building a large number in a variety of styles. Some of these saloon vehicles were transferred to the Isle of Wight where they survived until the end of steam there in 1966. On the mainland many 'Birdcage' sets (so called because of their raised guards' lookouts) included a saloon as their centre vehicle.

In photograph 1 (opposite upper) we see one such vehicle, S5449S, a semi-saloon non corridor lavatory composite coach in Birdcage 'Trio' set 587 at Lewes on 21st May 1952, in a Brighton bound train. 5449 was built in 1912 as SECR 1208 by the Metropolitan R.C.&W., one of a batch of 29 similar coaches which became SR Diagram 315. It was 60ft long and comprised four 3rd class (originally 2nd) compartments nearest the camera, followed by a 1st class saloon seating nine, followed by two 1st class compartments. The saloon and the nearer of the first class compartments each had access to a lavatory. This coach is probably still in Southern Green livery. It was withdrawn along with its fellows, in the second half of the 1950s. The other vehicles in set 587 were Brake Third 3420 and Lavatory Brake Third 3492.

Photograph 2 (opposite lower) is of First class saloon S7347, carrying BR red livery at Redhill on 22nd June 1952. This was one of 11 such vehicles built for the SECR by Metropolitan R.C.&W in 1907 for Boat Train use. Originally numbered 939 by the SECR, it was 50ft long and had two first class compartments one end and one the other, with a saloon seating 12 in between. All compartments and the saloon had access to lavatories. The SECR was very keen on tailoring the design of its coaches to the services on which they were intended to run, hence the multiplicity of variations in nominally similar coaches. However, some coaches such as this one did not last very long on their intended workings. Not permanently allocated to a set it had certainly joined the pool of 'loose' coaches in SR days. It was renumbered 7347 by the Southern, becoming Diagram 490 and was withdrawn in July 1956. The train shown here is interesting, with a Maunsell 'Restriction 4' Brake on one side and what looks like an ex LSWR style coach on the other. Such mixed formations were unusual for the tidy minded Southern, even in BR days and one wonders where the train was going. A scratch formation of stock on an excursion to Brighton or an inter-regional train to Dover perhaps?

Photograph 3 (below) shows an ex SECR saloon in Departmental use; a not uncommon end as the saloon provided useful 'Mess' or Office space. This vehicle was built as SECR 3786 in 1905 as a strengthening vehicle for the Royal Train. It eventually became SR First Saloon No. 7920 in 1925 and was the sole vehicle to Diagram 619. Its probable use would have been on 'Race day' specials and other excursions. Converted to a 'service vehicle' in 1948 it was renumbered 1062S and is seen here at Wimbledon serving as a mobile office along with several other interesting vehicles.

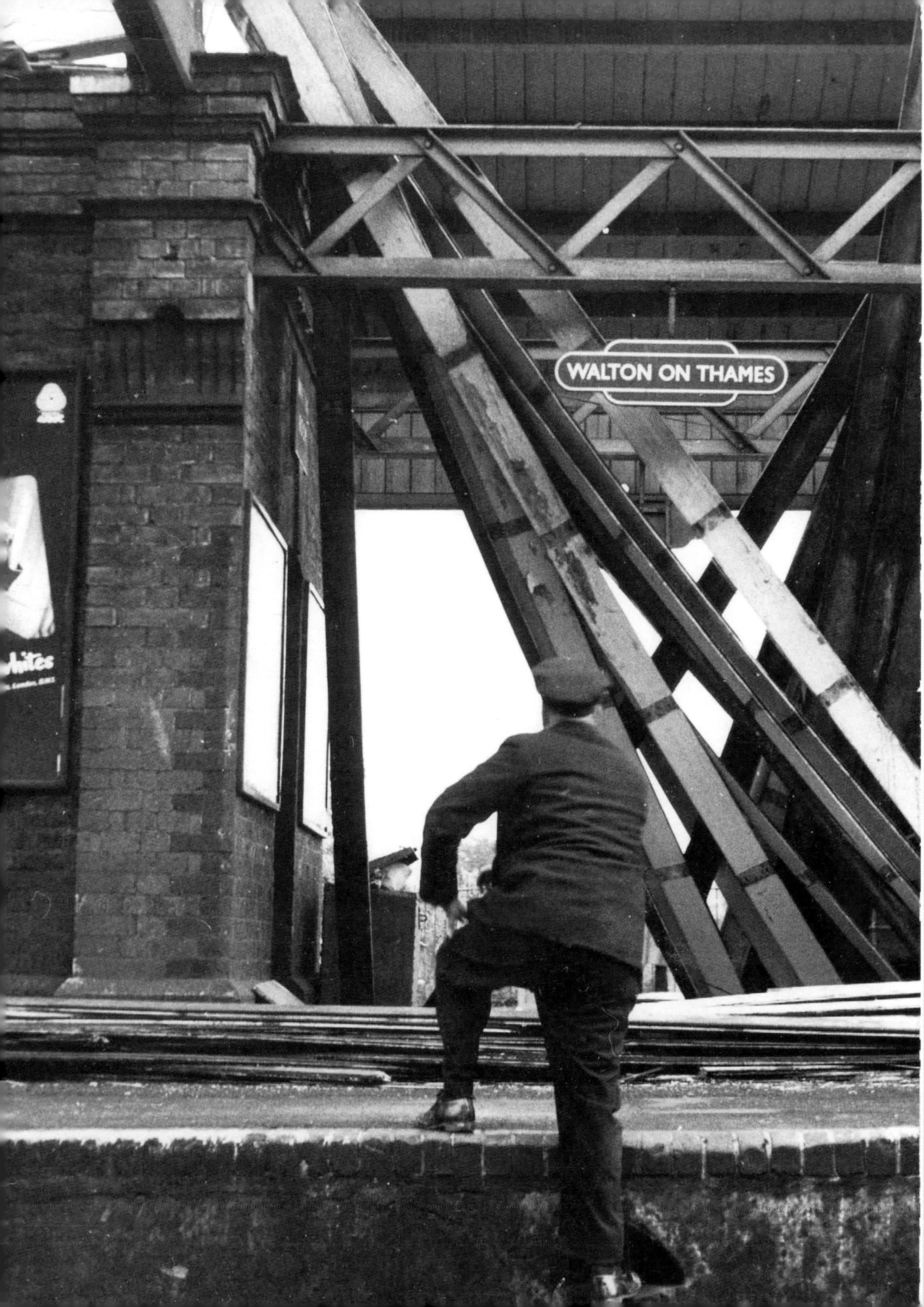
WALTON ON THAMES

No excuses for more from Rod Hoyle. That to the left needs no explanation although the thoughts of the railwayman seeing what was the canopy on the island platform of his old station demolished around him can perhaps only be imagined.

Above Rod has captured what he himself describes as ".. the shunter standing to attention." The location is Winchester City and the train is leaving for Waterloo around 9.00 am in April 1965 behind 35007 'Aberdeen Commonwealth'. This was one of the services on which the senior businessmen on their way to the 'City' would travel, the positions they held meaning their presence would not be required until late morning. Then time for lunch, perhaps another meeting in the afternoon and home before the rush. Rod likened the pose to the soldier standing sentry duty - ready for inspection. Below - different poses passing Salisbury shed, Ron Piercey and steam-raiser Percy Pittman.

September 1966 - not a good month

September 1966 was not a good month for the Southern Region. With electrification work on the south western main line already affecting services, the same division was seemingly plagued with a number of incidents, all intended to cause the maximum difficulty to an already beleaguered railway attempting to modernise and yet still maintain services.

At least five incidents are known of. The first occurred at Eastleigh on 1st September and involved the 18.48 Southampton to Eastleigh freight service. As was usual, this arrived from Southampton and then ran through the station to wait on the up through line before propelling back into the goods yard. Unfortunately on this occasion there appeared to be some confusion in the East Signal Box, so instead of taking the route into the yard the route was set into Platform 4 which was also already occupied by two diesel units, Nos 1109/33, both with the brakes hard on and ready to form the 20.09 to Portsmouth. The results were obvious. The brake van of the freight was 'practically demolished' whilst several other wagons were badly damaged, rearing up in the process. In consequence part of the station verandah was also brought down. The only other damage was to the two diesel units although this was, in fact, limited and both were back in service within a few days.

The next known incident was on the following day, 2nd September and this time near Crowthorne. Here, part of the 09.14 Blisworth to Redhill van train became derailed. Both lines were blocked and normal working not resumed until mid-day on the 3rd.

There was now a gap of just over two weeks until 20th September when it was the turn of a new Electro-Diesel, No E6037 to 'fall off' at Clapham Junction. The locomotive had only been new to service on 3rd July.

Then on 28th September comes the subject of the accompanying photograph. Mark Abbott had just ridden up from Brockenhurst to Waterloo on 35003* and was now with the engine running tender first back to Nine Elms. Seen from the cab was this view of Standard Class 3, No 82023 embedded in the rear of 2-Hal unit, 2626, which had been stood at signals between Waterloo and Vauxhall. The force of the collision pushed the electric set forward by some 15 feet, whilst also derailing the rear coach of the unit. There is some slight conflict reference the electric unit, one report referring to it being a Windsor local working whilst another comments it was an empty set destined for Wimbledon Park.

The Nine Elms breakdown crane attended with 73037, whilst 80154 was later used to haul the damaged unit to Clapham Junction, where it was reported as still standing some weeks later on 12th November. 82023 was released and arrived back at Nine Elms under its own power at 14.50, although this would be its last time in steam, as it was had suffered a fractured right hand steam pipe in the collision and was condemned a few days later. Other damage involved the buffer beam, although Mark commented this was not too bad. There was also damage to the footplate framing.

The line was cleared and re-opened to traffic around 16.30, just in time for the rush hour.

The month concluded with D6535 running through the catch points at the north end of the loop at Weston, just south of Micheldever, whilst in charge of the 19.53 Redbridge to Feltham freight. The engine ended up in soft ground and was not eventually recovered until 9th October.

* Mark Abbott's notes on the trip refer to the service as 07.37 from Brockenhurst, arriving 09.42 at Waterloo - nine minutes late. Even so and due to the number of slacks referred to below, it was not a bad performance. "At the time and possibly due to the newness of the (Southampton) Airport Station, I was noting passengers on and off: just one on and one off in this case, a bit different now!" "There were speed restrictions for track work (points and crossings), of 15 mph at Redbridge, also below Wallers Ash Tunnel, at Wallers Ash Distant (points and crossings), at Winchfield (points and crossings) and finally at Berrylands, the latter a 40 mph slack".

35003 is referred to as steaming well throughout but the riding was 'a bit lively', with the boiler loose at the back end and the cab shaking a bit. This may explain why the engine received a 'NC - Non classified' repair at Eastleigh from 5th January 1967.

Notes by Mark Abbott, with reference to 'The Railway Observer', 'Railway Magazine' and Bill Bishop.

This page, snapshots from the window of a passing train at Wallers Ash.

D6535 is seen in the dirt at the north end of the up loop having failed to stop.

Having ended up in soft ground, mechanical damage was fortunately limited although the lightweight panelling of the rear can suffered. This was mainly due to impact with the brake van marshalled next to the engine and visible along with various wagons next to the engine.

Photos: Mark Abbott.

Not mentioned in the text as we have no detail as to exactly when in September 1966 it occurred, was a delay to the down 'Bournemouth Belle', caused by a hot axle box on one of the cars.

June 1955 had not been good either...

June 1955 the time of the ASLEF strike.

It lasted just under two weeks and caused, according to some reports, permanent damage to the rail network, with customers, both freight and passenger alike, seeking out and then remaining with alternative means of transport - invariably road. Whatever the political ramifications the strike caused, there were likewise difficulties at the various works, Eastleigh included, where the works driver and fireman were absent and consequently there quickly built up a backlog of overhauled locomotives cluttering the shops.

This was the scene at the top of No 2 bay on 14th June 1955, just a few hours before the dispute was eventually settled. Visible are just a few of the 15 locomotives on which work had been completed in the previous two weeks and now ready to be re-united with tenders (where appropriate, of course) and taken back into service.

The list was (together with the type of repair undertaken), from left to right, 35010 - intermediate, 30488 - general, 76019 - intermediate, 30937 - general, 34069 - general, 30532 - intermediate. Other engines similarly completed and awaiting exit at the same time were, 76012 - intermediate, 30346 - intermediate, 30767 - general, 30112 - general, 30783 - general, 34058 - general, 30518 - general, 30850 - general, and 42081 - casual repair.

In the centre is a tray used when stripping engines. Small components would be placed inside and the whole thing lifted and then placed in the 'bosh' - acid / soda cleaning tank. Behind are a number of new springs.

Notice also, 35010 still retains its ribbed casing.

Photograph - Mark Abbott.

Permanent Way Notes by Graham Hatton

WATERLOO STATION
relaying of switches and crossings approaching Platforms 1 to 7, 1954.

In order to ensure that new track layouts were relaid with the minimum inconvenience to the travelling public, they were built up away from the site, or as in this case away from the city, before the weekend relaying dates. This is a very time consuming occupation. The components would be manufactured elsewhere and brought together on this pre-assembly site. Much material was imported through Redbridge (Southampton). Hardwood timbers, when used, would come from abroad; softwood timbers and sleepers would be cut and treated at Redbridge, by pressure impregnation with creosote.

As with many layouts built at this time and for many years to come, the track is bullhead design. The introduction of full depth cast crossings for the bisected scissors crossover seen here has made use of evolving technology to cast complex crossing areas in units and avoids much of the complexity and associated wear resulting from building these crossings from separate components.

The layout can also be fitted with much of the signalling equipment for activating the new points at this stage. It is then numbered up on all rail joints, timbers etc., before being reduced to either units of track or switch and crossing units and timbers for transport, in this case by train to site.

With all the rails cut to length, chairs fitted to timbers etc., the subsequent reassembly of the layout on site is a much quicker operation.

The two views show a portion of the new layout and will be seen from the approach to Waterloo end looking into the station. Platform 1 would be on the right.

Good views of full depth cast crossings used in this situation and the building up of track are also seen in the Preview Issue of 'The Southern Way', dealing with Lewisham.

On site and the train bringing the material stands to the right of the layout being renewed. Its 700 class loco and crew patiently await the next instruction. Cranes seen in the picture had a relatively small working radius and the material trains would need to shunt round the layouts in many cases several times, to minimise crane movements. Alternatively the crane would need to travel back and forth with both old and new material, but this takes longer. Work planning would take into account the need to have a track to work off both for the material train and the crane. Sometimes it was necessary to relay panels of track temporarily for the crane and material trains to work off, this still being the case today. The relaying of such a large volume of track would take place over a number of weekends, sometimes this would present challenges to the operating department, as lines would be left disconnected between weekends, but in this case it appears all was reconnected between weekends.

This is a component renewal, the days of digging formations and reballasting were still a way off, so the old ballast has been manually dug out to the sleeper bottom and dumped in adjacent areas and track ready for reuse. Some 'topping up' of ballast will then follow. The old material has been removed, but this appears to be a 'like for like' as opposed to a remodelling style relaying, the old conductor rail will be reused on new con rail porcelain pots with little amendment. The complex full depth cast crossings are evident here. There is still much manual adjustment to be made even though the layout is pre-fabricated.

To the left a 'T' spanner is being used to tighten some chairscrews. The check rail in the foreground is about to be held in place with the bar to key it up. In time honoured tradition behind the crane 'runner wagon' a couple of inspectors stand on the rails looking at progress and giving instructions. The photos of the relaying were taken in May 1954 and judging by the coats they are wearing it was not a hot May!

The track to the left of the picture has all been relaid, that on the right is original and connections between new and old are in the foreground. Note the full depth crossing made to match the adjacent BH rail. The piece of equipment on top of the rail in the foreground looks like a rail adjuster. This was a device to slightly move rails longitudinally to line up fishplate holes by opening or closing a rail joint, and hence the man leaning over the other end of the rail is probably allowing this rail gap here to be opened slightly using the adjuster on the other rail end. 9th May 1954.

Top - There is much activity in this photo. The steam crane unloads the next components from the material train. The new track is to the right and the diamond, slip and track to the left are the originals. Despite the various people looking at work rather than doing it, all would have a role. This type of work is physically demanding and requires standing up straight periodically and also considering the next move! The trilby hats spread around the site indicate a visitation from the 'top brass'!

Relaying sites at this stage often made you wonder if it would all come together, but it always did, Monday would come and the operating department would require it!

Most problems were small ones like wide fishplate joints, which would be overcome with some slackening and adjusting of other rails and components. Careful planning and measuring in the weeks before would see that all the components arrived and that they were loaded in the order in which they needed to be unloaded. The 'cutting in point' would be marked and squared up along with offset information. You did not want to start off from the wrong place, or too far along! Material trains were arranged carefully and normally different consists for each stage, the old removed material either being loaded away at the start or loaded onto the now emptied material train.

Below - Seen from above the work appears clearer. Platforms 1 and 2 on the left have their new approach track laid. The old track under the crane will await relaying until the next shift. A wing rail for a diamond awaits lifting from the train, possibly that missing in the previous picture. Crossings lie in the 'four-foot' ready for moving. Material storage has made much use of the space to the left of the approach tracks. The P/Way gang seem to be working on the tandem turnout and the S&T have started on the fitting up of the points from Platform 2. The ballast dug out from between the timbers of Platform 2's switches and crossovers into the adjacent Platform 3 track will be returned before topping up. The 'C' speed restriction boards are in place at the platform end, more a formality here as the speed is only low anyway. The train formation is worthy of note too, with the rear parked out of site in Platform 4. It includes two vans, probably also used for the conveyance of staff to site before the days of road vehicles for staff. Then there is an open wagon for all the small stuff such as fishplates, keys etc., before the bogie flats for all the main material such as rail and crossings. The crane would normally be brought to site with its runner wagon and mess van formed in this train and often had the required red lamp hung from the coupling whilst working on the site. 9th May 1954.

Above - It is three days later now and the track is in full use. Given the curving situation of the site, the need to access all platforms in this group from the up and down slow lines and the need for 'parallel moves' wherever possible, to increase the operating potential of the layout, it was necessary to employ a lot of the more complex P Way formations. This is a heavily used formation like most track at Waterloo and regular relaying here is an almost continuous process. Twenty years use out of this relaying would be considered good, but many smaller components would be replaced within this period due to excessive wear. Some staff are still working on odd components and material is left ready for the next weekend to the left of the site and on the platform, a practice frowned on even then. To the right is 35015.

Left - Two months further on, 28th July 1954, and there is almost no sign that anything has happened. Note even Waterloo had a garden alongside the track at that time. The engines, a 'Lord Nelson' and Urie 4-6-0, are no doubt making their way back to Nine Elms.

'REBUILDING' - THE LETTERS AND COMMENTS PAGE

No sooner had Issue No 1 hit the shelves than literally the following day we received a telephone call reference the Ramsgate photographs. It appears at least one may have appeared in the solitary 'Bedside Backtrack' volume of a few years ago. My apologies, I do not have a copy handy. (More recently an excellent article but with more photographs and information on the same incident has appeared in the issue No 17 of 'Railway Archive'.)

We have also had a suggestion that the view of the ladies painting could well be Chandlers Ford, very close to Eastleigh, certainly not confirmed as such but the best idea so far.

Many of you have also taken the trouble to write and telephone with comments, (dare I say, mostly positive), thank you all.

One letter from a regular friend to 'SW' comes from Fred Emery. Fred raises a number of questions I cannot answer on the rebuilding of 35018 - hopefully Mark Abbott will be able to respond in due course, but he also comments in other areas as follows, " In the article on 'The Brighton Belle', it mentions the naming of the Pullmans. I was told some time ago by a manager of the Pullman Car Co., that the choice of names came about after mulling over some of the original names from LBSCR days, these though were rejected. Then came the idea of naming the cars after the ladies working in the Pullman offices."

Fred also enquired if Mark Abbott might have ever heard of the suggestion to place a Bulleid boiler on a 'Britannia' chassis? I have asked Mark Abbott the question and he was unable to assist. However, and not to be beaten, I then asked the same question of Eric Best a former Eastleigh Fitter - Eric's memoirs will be appearing in 'SW' in the not too distant future. He did recall some discussion on this but was again unaware as to why it was not acted upon. (Possibly, at the time this was being considered, more steam experiments were not deemed worthwhile - Ed.) As Eric commented, "...weight was not the problem, the steel firebox was lighter then copper anyway. Remember too the Bulleid's were not the only ones to use a steel firebox as this material was also used for those ***** Austerity things."

Thanks Eric and Fred, it is memories and comments such as these that make the whole 'SW' project worthwhile.

Also from John Bruce comes comment on the article "New Stock for the Eastleigh Breakdown Crane", Issue No 1, page 54. The lamps, he states, are Tilley floodlight projector lamps, not acetylene lamps. "It was just a big version of an ordinary Tilley but with a silver coloured reflector. A little meths burner to pre-heat the mantle, pump up the pressure in the tank (paraffin), open the vale and away you go - lots of light."

Possibly, though, the most comment pertaining to Issue No 1 concerns the view of the Brighton Works cat. Yes we all know cats and railways were often inseparable but most of the time these were unofficial visitors, inhabiting stations, signal boxes and the like. Indeed this on the subject and again from Fred Emery, "....they were found everywhere, offices, signal-boxes, goods depots, works etc. Perhaps sadly as modernisation did away with so much of the railway heritage, it was to be expected that they to would became a lesser part of the scene. I can always recall attending a meeting in an office and on selecting a chair (it was also potentially the most comfortable), being told - 'not that one it's the cats chair."

I was also advised that at Fratton there was at least one cat officially on the pay-roll. Referred to as 'Cat 3', it was allocated to the depot and paid 1/- per week for milk. It did, though, have to catch its own food. Straight away one wonders where were cats '1' and '2' allocated, and did each have to have a shed code attached in case it went wandering? Spurious I know, but all good clean fun.

Of course we could then digress into the subject of railway dogs, and there were many of these, mainly, I realise, stuffed but serving a valid purpose collecting for charity. An article on the subject would be most welcome if anyone fancies having a go.

Finally, thanks to Peter Bailey, Dave Hammersley, he of 'Roxey Mouldings' fame, for reading the text and Bruce Murray, photographic genius.

Please do send your comments good or otherwise, they will all be read and responded to.

Next page: The Southern Railway opened two suburban lines in Surrey from 1929 onwards and both in two stages. The first was between Wimbledon and South Merton in July 1929, extended six months later to a junction at Sutton. Then in 1938 came a junction at Motspur Park for a new line to Tolworth, serving the ever expanding growth of 'suburbia'. This line too was extended further from Tolworth through to Chessington South in May 1939, although the planned eventual extension to Leatherhead was never completed..
At noon on 16th June 1936, work was in progress for the new junction on the existing line at Motspur Park, with the erection of the bracket signal for the new line.

Getty Images / Harry Todd / Stringer 3396611

(We are in the early stages of planning for a feature on the new lines in a later issue.)

Weedkilling Trains
Notes by Graham Hatton

The weedkiller train passes on one of the many branch lines. Weedkiller trains have been in use for many years prior to and since this photo was taken in 1949 on an unknown piece of line. There main function has always been the killing off of weeds in the area of the ballast and immediate cess. Weeds allowed to grow in the ballast, apart from looking unsightly, will clog the ballast thus affecting its drainage. Once established many weeds spread rapidly in this environment.

Today weed spraying trains still run and perform the same basic function, though some of the chemicals used are considerably more friendly than the residual chemicals used at that time.
In addition, 'scrub spraying' is also now carried out from the train where required, which keeps in check undergrowth such as brambles at the side of the cess. The equipment used for this is still a jet form, often directed manually by the crew.

In the photo the train appears to be being propelled, judging by the headboard and lack of lamp, so the driver would be the man in the middle. The train had its own crew, who, as can be seen from the way they are directing the weed spraying nozzles in the photo, could make adjustments as required on each side. The booms rotate out of the way to pass platforms and underbridges etc., as in the operational position they are well 'out of gauge'.
Weedkilling trains were often a collection of old tank wagons and converted vans and coaches, and for many years on the Southern Region the work was carried out by contracts with such firms as Chipman's of Horsham, who maintained the vehicles.

This photo taken with the previous one shows the van ready for its next move on 7th April 1949; at this stage it was run by the Engineer's Department of the Southern Region. This is the traditional time of the start of the season for weed spraying. Before the summer really got going the train would visit all the running lines, branches and principal sidings on the system, which was no small undertaking. It required a great deal of train planning to slot in its relatively slow speed on parts of the busy system in the hours of daylight.

The various arrangements for spraying are clearly visible here, as are the cable and chain mechanisms for raising the boom sprays. Note also the connections to the water tanks, in this case via the roof and the horn for attracting attention when propelling! It was not considered pleasant to be weedsprayed, though many 'lived' to tell the tale!

377306
FIRST SOUTHERN ELECTROSTAR
TO ACHIEVE ½ MILLION MILES

Something a bit different, received just too late for Issue No 1. We have been approached by Chris Dodswell to see if we might mention the commemorative cover he has produced, proceeds from which will be given to 'The Rockinghorse Appeal' - the local Brighton Children's Hospital.

If you would like to assist in supporting this worthy cause Chris can be contacted at 330 Bexhill Road, St Leonards on Sea, East Sussex, TN38 8AL, or at chris.dodswell@southernrailway.com

Inevitably all those sprays required some sophisticated pumping equipment and a healthy water supply from the adjacent tank wagons, which often made use of old loco tenders. There would normally also be some large tanks in which the chemicals used would be poured from sacks and mixed with the water.

The view shows well the functional nature of such adapted vehicles, in this case gas lit.

The above vehicle ran with a mess van as this was an all day job and would mean occasionally sitting it out in sidings awaiting the next booked move. The mess vans were functional (as were all railway vehicles at this time) providing basic seating, washing and cooking facilities.

An article on SR Weed killing Trains was featured in BRITISH RAILWAYS JOURNAL No 11, for Spring 1986.

The subject was also referred to in the SOUTHERN RAILWAY MAGAZINE for December 1931 and January 1932.

Weedspraying was considered important enough, even at this time, for some record of the activity to be made. This machine, possibly clockwork driven, recorded by graphical means the mileage of the run and the spraying of the cess, four foot and corresponding second cess or six foot between tracks.

Nowadays such records would be mandatory and include considerably more information than this, such as the chemicals used and their strength to give a dosage rate. Nevertheless in 1949 this was a good start - at a time when early chemicals, by their nature, had quite a long lasting effect!

Above: The up side platform and shelter at Monks Lane Halt looking towards Oxted and London. This was an LBSCR railcar halt opened on 1ˢᵗ July 1907, in the hope of anticipated residential development on the line from Eridge. The halt closed on 11ᵗʰ September 1939 and is seen here surviving intact some years later on 24ᵗʰ August 1947.

Below: The downside shelter and nameboard at Monks Lane Halt, 24ᵗʰ August 1947.

Above: We now move south and east to the line between Groombridge and Tunbridge Wells. High Rocks Halt was opened on 1st June 1907 although this time with no other intention other than affording passengers the opportunity to enjoy the nearby countryside. The staggered platforms were both accessed from the overbridge and the up platform is depicted on 13th September 1950. With the long flight of stairs there was no chance of disabled access here!
Below: The opposite, down platform. The halt was closed on 5th May 1952.   All - Terry Cole collection

PRODUCTION LINE BUILDING OF ALL STEEL ELECTRIC STOCK EASTLEIGH 1946

In late 1946, the Southern Railway produced a small number of booklets describing the "Line Production Methods Employed in the Manufacture of all Steel Electric Stock". A number of photographs were included as well as plans of stages of assembly through the shops.

Unit No 4111 illustrated was the first of its type and although coming under the coverall designation of '4-SUB' they differed from the slightly earlier '4101' class - Nos 4101-4110, in not having domed front ends. The sets were specifically designed with only eight compartments per motor coach, which allowed for slightly more room for standing passengers and more leg room for those sitting if no standees were present.

The justification for this was simply that it had been recognised that some passengers will invariably prefer to travel at the front of the train, in the belief they will be able to alight quicker even if there happened to be empty seats elsewhere in the set. The two trailers were of nine and ten compartments respectively, with a four coach set

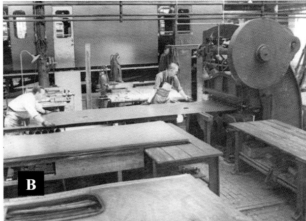

Views 'A' through to 'F' on this page deal with the construction of the roof.

A - The sheet metal shop and shearing of the roof panels
B - In the same shop, punching roof panels.

C - Steel body erecting shop, joining roof panels by spot welding.
D - In the same location as C, this is assembly and welding of the roof on a jig.

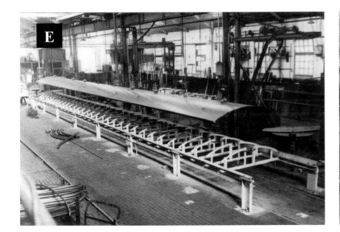

Nos E and F are also in the steel body erecting shop, with E showing the completed roof being lifted from the jig, whilst in F there is a view of the underside of the roof, revealing the carlines.

weighing 142 tons and able to accommodate 420 seated passengers. The nine coach trailer was produced should 1st class re-introduced at a later date.

As a means of ensuring maximum capacity, six-aside seating was provided, which was reported as 'sampled' by the General Manager and his entourage at Eastleigh. To be honest though a brief sampling of very senior posteriors, placed for a short time in the compartment, was hardly the same as a sardine type journey under normal conditions. Nevertheless the

comfort stakes were considered suitable and ten four car sets, Nos 4111 - 4120 were completed at Eastleigh in 1946. A second batch of identical units numbered 4364 to 4376, was built in 1947.

The booklet also only deals with the bodywork, with no mention of the underframes. Research reveals these may have been made at any one of the three Southern works, Eastleigh, Lancing, or possibly even Ashford, possibly more than one works having been involved.

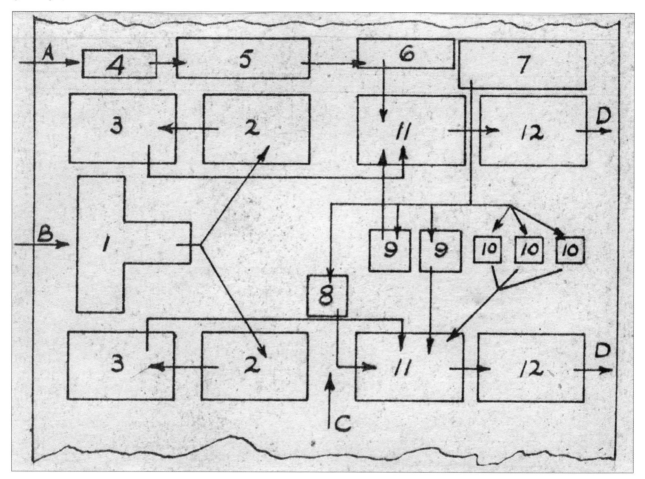

Within the same book were two plans describing the assembly area within the Eastleigh Carriage Works. (Note - there is correlation between the letters on the above plan and those used to identify the photographs within this article.)

1	Spot welder for joining roof panels.	**7**	Spot welder for details on coach end, motor end and quarter jigs.
2	Roof jigs.	**8**	Motor end assembly and welding jig.
3	Roof racks.	**9**	Coach end jigs.
4	Spot welders for details on quarters.	**10**	Motor end quarter jig.
5	Mobile quarter jigs.	**11**	Main assembly jigs.
6	Stacking ground for quarters.	**12**	Fitting and welding bays (then to finishing production line.)
A	Input of panels for quarter jigs.	**C**	Input of details for motor end jigs.
B	Input of panels for roof jigs.	**D**	Output of finished coach shell.

Still within the steel body erecting shop, left - jig assembly and welding of the motorman's cab. Lower left - jig assembly and welding of coach side quarters. Lower right - main assembly of coach sides and roof.

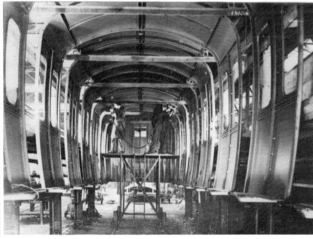

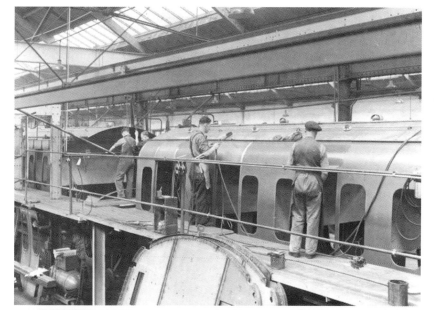

Opposite - Body finishing production line, diagram of layout.

Left - Steel body erecting shop, erection of coach end and jointing of door head panels, main assembly jig.

Centre - View of body welded to underframe.

Body finishing production line - general view.

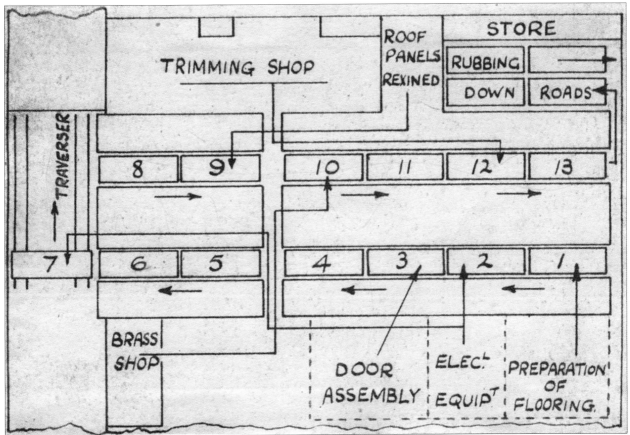

1	Lay floors - fix switch boxes - paint ends outside	8	Rexine partitions, fit roof packings and seat brackets. Fill and stop.
2	Wire switch boxes.	9	Hang ceilings and elbow pressings, paint roof.
3	Hang doors, paint ends inside.	10	Fix light quarters, net racks and mirrors. Apply filling coat.
4	Fix partitions and seat angles - rexine pillars - paint roof and ends.	11	Fix heaters and seat rials. Stop and apply filling coat, paint roof.
5	Fix lights, paint roof inside.	12	Fix seats and backs, lay lino.
6	.Fix door checks, paint roof outside.	13	Clean inside, stain. (Then to Paint Shop.)
7	Paint inside roof and sides, first filling coat outside. Wire for heaters		

Body finishing production line, sub-assembly of doors.

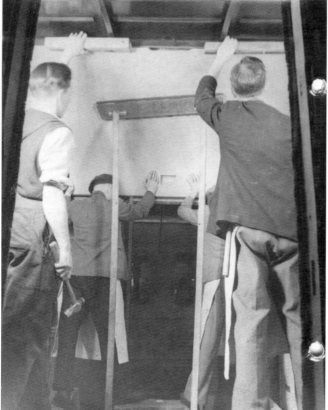

Above - Body finishing production line, hanging steel doors.

Left - Body finishing production line, erecting pre-formed ceiling panels.

Below - Body finishing production line, interior panels clipped into position.

Interior third-class compartment. (The number 19 appearing on the print is a slight puzzle, as the booklet only contained 18 views, all of which have been reproduced here.)

Technical Details.	
Length Overall.	62 ft. 6 ins.
Width.	9 ft. 0 ins.
Weight of roof above rail level.	12 ft. 4½ ins.
Centre of bogies.	44 ft. 0 ins.
Total power of motors.	480 horse power.
Average tare weight (4-car unit).	35.35 tons.
Average number of seats per vehicle (4-car unit).	105
Average weight of coach per passenger (4-car unit).	758 lbs.

Whilst as stated at the start of this article, the booklet is clearly dated November 1946, construction actually took place some time earlier, with the 'Railway Observer' for August 1946 commenting, "The new four car Suburban units are being put into traffic at the rate of one complete unit per week. Units 4111-20 have been noted in traffic, and are believed to be working from Orpington with units 4101-10….".

In total 35 new 4-coach sets of similar type were constructed by the Southern prior to nationalisation, together with 116 further trailer vehicles used to augment existing sets. In all of these the body side painting was continued up to roof level, as seen in the illustration on page 90. Between the vehicles, large self contained buffers were fitted, The units were also fitted with the standard English Electric equipment used by the SR.

Later 4-sub units, whilst externally almost identical, varied in the type of electrical equipment fitted, Unit 4130 for example, had a new type of ventilated lightweight traction motor. Additionally the provision for

Above - A later 4-sub motor coach, with detail differences compared with that seen on page 82. On this vehicle there is an additional ventilation duct on the roof above the guard's compartment, which was provided in connection with the lightweight traction motor fitted. Notice also the variation in handrail detail on both side and end together with the droplight alteration. This particular vehicle was recorded on 18th February 1949, probably at Eastleigh although this cannot be confirmed. Aside from the livery alteration, the position of the individual vehicle number is still identical with that in SR days.

Collection: John Wenyon

Right - Completed underframes. Unfortunately the location is not recorded, but, as stated in the text it could well be any of the SR works, although perhaps Lancing is the most likely.

Finally a series of snapshots from the camera of the late Arthur Tayler. Nos '1' and '2' are of units 4114 and 4115 respectively. Both were recorded at Selhurst, with the former clearly under test. Although undated these are likely to have when brand new. Slightly later, No '3' is of 4-SUB No 4364 and No '4' 4379, again at Selhurst. (Incidentally unit No. 4382, completed around October 1948 was the last to have the 'British Railways' wording painted on the front.) Lastly at '5' is the interior layout of the later sets modified from all compartment to the '3+2 ' arrangement.

first-class was dispensed with and a second 10-compartment trailer included. Following market research, however, the two motor coaches and one of the trailers were designed with a centre gangway rather than all compartments. Whilst this reduced the seating capacity, standing room was increased, with the added bonus of easier access to the doors.

By the September 1946 issue of the 'R.O', correspondents were reporting that sets 4121/2 had been completed as part of a batch of ten further units. Assuming the sets were completed in unit order, Nos 4129/30 were reported as having been completed in the December issue.

With thanks to Ray Chorley and Adrian Swain for providing the basic material for this article.

Upper left - The cab of 35005 modified with the stoker attachment At the same time as the fitting of the stoker a Flaman speed recorded was also installed.

Above - The boiler / firebox (No 1091) fitted to 35005, either prepared for or having just undergone steam test. The firebox orifice is of a vertically elongated shape compared with the standard Pacific type.

Lower left - a view of the delivery chute, also with the 'Ajax' firehole doors seen in the open position. This enabled hand-firing to take place if required, although these half doors were only controllable by hand. To the right of the door, the five hand-wheels controlled the donkey engine on the tender and also the steam jets intended to direct coal within the firebox.

Opposite page - A close up of the tender donkey engine for driving the screw and also the screw itself. Although undated this was likely to have been taken at the time of fitting as there are no pieces of fuel apparent.

(A view of the complete tender front is shown on page 94.)

35005 'CANADIAN PACIFIC'

From the feedback we receive, one of the most popular features seems to be on the 'big engines'. With that in mind, then and conscious also of the need to give people what they want, we are delighted to present a small feature of new material reference the mechanical stoker fitted to 35005 during the period March 1948 to April 1951.

Several excellent accounts of the episode have already appeared * and we will not repeat the same information here.

Suffice to say that comments by a former Eastleigh fireman of the time, Hugh Abbinett, provide the basis for that new material, even if they are not particularly complimentary concerning the modification. Hugh recalls the crews were issued with what in effect was am oversize 'tuning fork' intended to assist should coal become jammed. The oft quoted problem also arose in that the coal issued varied in size and consequently jams were frequent. When this happened, also, the donkey engine on the tender would overhead. When questioned as to whether the screw could be reversed to assist in freeing a jam, Hugh was adamant that it was not possible on this engine.

As he also put it, "...coal would arrive in various sizes, some pieces the size of a fist were ideal, but other pieces were the size of a man....we would spend far more time in the tender trying to break it up into manageable pieces than under normal circumstances...". "Then there was the problem with firing. Rarely was the coal delivered to exactly where it was needed on the firebed and either we had to resort to hand firing or she just went 'off the boil' - usually both."

Further new information also reveals that the basis of the whole concept may have originated with Stephen Townroe in an alleged conversation with Bulleid. Townroe is supposed to have commented that a modern design (referring to what were then the new Pacifics) needed a new approach to firing. Certainly this is exactly the type of innovation Bulleid was keen on, although, as is known it took far longer to secure the actual equipment, due to the constraints of the period, than had originally been intended.

Even so the *Southern Region Magazine* for August 1948 included a photograph of the engine in its new guise leaving Waterloo at the head of the 'Devon Belle' and accompanied by several column inches of text describing its features. When working 35005, crews were often accompanied by a locomotive inspector as well as a representative from the manufacturer

In late February 1950, and after four months at Eastleigh Works, 35005 was released to traffic, with the intention of conducting monitored trails between Clapham Junction and Salisbury. This involved bagged coal, no doubt of suitable size, being fed by hand into the stoker from the tender by two men who had the misfortune to travel in the tender bunker although a tarpaulin was fitted. (Possibly a tarpaulin was present from the outset - see photo on next page.) Even so it must have been a hellish environment, the choice between draught and dust or darkness - as well, no doubt, as draught. The stoker was removed and the engine reverted to hand-firing from late April 1951.

A Flaman speed recorded was also fitted to 35005 at the same time as the stoker.

* The mechanical stoker is referred to in some detail in, 'Bulleid Power' by A J Fry, also 'Bulleids Pacifics', by D W Winkworth, D L Bradley in 'Locomotives of the Southern Railway Part 2', and 'The Book of the Merchant Navy Pacifics', by Richard Derry.

Left - Concluding the few words on 35005, is a view of the complete tender, No 3115, on 18th March 1948. The position of the donkey engine and screw are also seen in context compared with the close up on the previous page. Compared also with the similar view of a standard tender, as depicted in the 'Merchant Navy' article which featured in the Preview Issue of 'SW', one noticeable omission is the holders for ARP tin-hats. Notice also the electric light fitting,, possibly unique to this tender. The doors accessing the bunker are obvious although no doubt there was considerable risk of a deluge of coal onto the footplate if these were opened to clear a jam when the tender was full. The whole process of resolving such difficulties was made more onerous as the screw would have been buried at this point.

Only one tender was modified in this way and consequently, when 35005 was out of action for some time for repair or breakdown, as indeed did take place on at least two occasions, the tender too was idle and could not be matched with another engine of the class. The two tone paintwork is interesting, but was probably only provided for the benefit of clarity of the photograph.

Below - As is often the case, no sooner had we gone to press with the 'Diesel Special' on 10201-3 (see inside cover for more details), than this view turned up from the collection of Mark Abbott and taken by J S Griffiths. 10201 is shown at the hitherto unphotographed - well, from a diesel perspective at least, location of Lyndhurst Road and heading for Bournemouth with the down 'Belle', on 16th March 1952.

...and speaking of steam versus diesel, the following was printed in the Southern Region Magazine in 1948 , at a time when main line diesel power was in its infancy. (The LMS engines were working but it would be a further three years before 10201 would appear.)

" Locomotivemen are so accustomed to noise when working their engines that is comes as something in the nature of a surprise, when it is mentioned as to a recommendation of a certain type. The tests which are being carried out with different engines on 'foreign' lines * has let a number of readers to send us comments on the Southern Railway 'West Country' class; and the comparison of one reader, strangely enough, compares this 'steamer' with the new electric-diesel - to the latter's detriment. Here is the comment from one of our correspondents - 'The 'West Country' class was on a rising gradient, I could hear no exhaust noise - only the sound of the wheels on the rail. I always gave the palm to the GW 'King' in this respect, but the SR engine has it now. What a contrast to the Diesel uproar!"

* (The 1948 Locomotive Exchanges)

A TASTE OF...

...**things to come**, and we certainly don't mean we are going to start building fleets of 3-wheeled articulated railway vehicles. Instead I are delighted to report that, thanks to former Road Vehicle Inspector, Fred Emery, we have been given access to a large collection of photographs of Southern Railway / Region road vehicle views. Fred has also written copious notes on the fleet together with his own experiences, the result of which is probably the most detailed account yet produced from someone very much 'in the know'.

As an example and relative to this particular view, Fred comments, "A 3-ton Scammell Mechanical Horse, brand new in the Watford area and near to where the manufacturer was based. Unfortunately the tree obscures the name of the hospital, prohibiting a definite location. These vehicles had a one piece, horizontally opening screen across the cab front and a small splasher over the front wheel. For reasons that are not clear, most contemporary views of these vehicles show the splasher as a different colour to the main bodywork. The sidelights, if you can call them that, are the small protrusions hanging down from the door pillars. These were later repositioned much lower down, roughly in line with the top hinge of the side door. Initially and probably for most of their lives, no full side protection for the driver was provided. The single circular disc on the bodywork is the licence holder, although in service two further discs would be fitted for the carriers licences - one for the tractor and the other for the trailer. The white panel on the windscreen is probably an order number or clearance ticket from Scammell's. Later production models would have the figure '3' or '6' (the latter indicating 6-ton), on the front splasher assembly.

The body colour was dark green with white lettering, whilst, on this example, the chassis members appear to be black, later examples had both the chassis and wheel centres painted red.". The 'M' suffix referred to 'Motor'. On the trailer the two running numbers are present because the sides were removable, to provide for a flatbed trailer. They could (in theory, at least) be reunited at a later time. In service the registration number was usually carried just above the radiator.

A LOT MORE ON ROAD VEHICLES IN FUTURE ISSUES.

COLOUR INTERLUDE

One of the great pleasures in compiling 'Southern Way' is meeting new friends and viewing material previously hidden away for decades.

Bruce Oliver was recording the Southern scene, in both colour and black and white, from the early 1960s onwards and, whilst certain of his astounding views have appeared in 'Backtrack' in recent years, the rest have remained hidden away. (Look out for an album on electric traction by Bruce from Ian Allan in the near future, whilst we too will be producing an all colour steam title from Bruce in the Autumn of 2008.)

In the meantime and as taster of things to come, we have pleasure in presenting a small selection of scenes between Exeter and Yeovil in the period 1962-64.

Above - Having received attention from the Exmouth Junction cleaning staff, 'Z' 30955 stands in the middle road at Exeter St Davids awaiting the next train it will assist up the grade to Exeter Central. This particular engine had been employed on similar duties since 1958, for which task also it was eminently suitable. Bruce recorded this view in November 1962, at which time also the engine had just one month of life left, being withdrawn along the final members of the class at the end of the year.

Opposite top - The winter of 1962/63 will be recalled as ranking amongst one of the coldest in memory and it might well have been that '700' class No 30689 was, indeed, gainfully employed with its plough at that time. (Records report this engine as having been withdrawn, on paper at least, in November 1962, although it was not unknown for a machine to soldier on for a short time afterwards in case of need and assuming of course, it was mechanically sound.) The location is again Exmouth Junction, now the site of a supermarket complex.

Opposite lower - Alongside the Southern's shed at Exmouth Junction, 'N' class 2-6-0 No 31842 awaits its next turn of duty in company with an interloper from the Western Region. At this stage pannier tanks had been transferred to the former Southern depot to cover the banking turns previously undertaken by the 'Z' class, although the replacements were decidedly inferior. 19th January 1963.

Above - Moving east and the terminus at Seaton. Bruce recalls the day as being a bitterly cold Saturday in March 1963 - indeed as witness the solitary individual on the platform well wrapped up. 30048 is in the process of being watered, assuming of course the hose is not frozen? The crew also to have what appears to be an improvised side shutter in place whilst note too the lumps of coal resting on the cab roof. The profusion of pipe work from the buffer beam clearly show this was a motor fitted engine. 30048 remained in service until January 1964 whilst the branch itself closed in March 1966.

Freight working for a 'Merchant Navy'. 35010 'Blue Star', in charge of a westbound working, passing 'U' class 31798 on a similar duty at Yeovil Junction, 13ᵗʰ June 1964. Seeing a Pacific on freight was far more common on the West of England line compared with the Bournemouth line, although such duties were more usually milk trains. Possibly, then, 35010 is on an unbalanced working, certainly on a little more than a loose coupled service, as the front wagons at least would appear to be vacuum fitted.

Issue No 3 of *THE SOUTHERN WAY* (ISBN 978-1-906419-03-5) is due for release in Spring 2008 and will include another colour feature, permanent-way, locomotive and station photographs, as well as views from The Getty files.

Also included (space permitting), will be the first part of a major feature on the LSWR / Southern at Basingstoke, the Isle of Wight Railways in WW2, a collision between two Bulleids at Victoria and 'Push-Pull' to Alton from Hugh Abbinett.

Plus ………..(- some of things we promised last time (hopefully a branch line photo feature….)

To receive your copy the moment it is released, order in advance from your usual supplier, or direct from the publisher:

Kevin Robertson (Noodle Books) PO Box 279, Corhampton, SOUTHAMPTON, SO32 3ZX

Tel / Fax 01489 877880

www.kevinrobertsonbooks.co.uk